TORIANO GORDON, the chef behind Vegan Mob, grew up sharing soul food with his family and friends. When he began eating vegan, he was nostalgic for those childhood flavors, so he spent hours painstakingly re-creating them from scratch. His innovative dishes became the backbone of Vegan Mob, a Bay Area original that draws in vegans and carnivores alike.

Here he shares favorites from the restaurant as well as new recipes, inviting us to try crowd-pleasing favorites such as Brisket, Smackaroni, and Mobba'Q Baked Beans. In an homage to his youth in the Fillmoe (not Fillmore) and his San Francisco and Oakland communities, Toriano also draws inspiration from a multitude of cuisines with recipes such as La La Lumpia, Mafia Mobsta Noodles aka Garlic Noodles, Mob Lasagna, and Mob Taco Bowls—all made accessible for the home cook.

Vegan Mob also takes you out of the kitchen and into Toriano's life, highlighting his many family connections to the Bay Area and his bond with Bay Area rap and music. With inspirational advice, vibrant photographs, and tons of energy, *Vegan Mob* is an invitation for everyone to come to the table and enjoy a meal together.

VEGAN MOB

VEGAN BBQ & SOUL FOOD

VEGAN MOB

VEGAN BBQ & SOUL FOOD

TORIANO GORDON

WITH KORSHA WILSON

TEN SPEED PRESS
California | New York

PHOTOGRAPHS BY ED ANDERSON
ILLUSTRATIONS BY PHOTO DOCTOR GRAPHICS

CONTENTS

CHAPTER 5—
MOB FUSION

CHAPTER 6—
LET'S PARTY: FOOD, DRINKS, AND DESSERTS FOR A MOB

"VEGAN MOB COMPRISES ALL OF THE THINGS THAT INSPIRE ME:

A LOVE OF MY CITY, A LOVE OF HIP-HOP, AND, OF COURSE, A LOVE OF GOOD-ASS FOOD.

IT'S REBELLIOUS, IT'S GRITTY, IT'S REAL."

Vegan Mob, my vegan soul food restaurant in Oakland, California, is my favorite place in the world. The bright lime-green building facing Lake Park Ave., the smell of smoke as you walk up, the street art on the side of the building reading "it's the mob"—all of it makes me feel at home. It's where I spend the most time, where I test out new dishes, but most importantly, it's where I see my Bay Area community. On the days we're open, you'll often see a line of people waiting to place their order on the sidewalk right outside of our stand. There's old and young, vegans and nonvegans, all skin colors, all hair colors, everybody coming together to enjoy vegan barbecue in a space that reflects them and this neighbor-hood. It's beautiful. It's the Bay, and it's Oakland.

I've come a long way from selling plates of vegan barbecue and soul food out of my car and then at Bay Area farmers markets. It feels good to know that I'm running a business serving food inspired by the dishes that fed my soul for most of my life. Vegan dishes like macaroni and cheese—which we call Smackaroni and Cheese—gumbo, po' boys, and brisket are my direct line to the food that I grew up eating with my family. The only difference is I'm serving them without animal products, making them a little healthier but still keeping the heart of the dishes intact.

Since I opened Vegan Mob in 2019, the Oakland community has really embraced me and my version of comfort food. The base of the menu may be American classics, but the flavors blend influences from a lot of the cultures you see here in the city. I use ingredients and techniques from my family's classic soul food recipes, as well as Asian, Latin, and Caribbean cooking to create Vegan Mob's plant-based dishes, because those communities have impacted this area, and those ingredients are readily available to me here. In the Vegan Mob kitchen, I experiment with plant-based ingredients, remixing them to create meat-free versions of dishes from those cultures, creating food that is big on flavor—and I don't stop remixing until I get it just right.

Part of the reason why I think Vegan Mob has been received so well by the neighborhood and customers is because the restaurant also reflects me, and I'm a product of the Bay Area. Vegan Mob and my music are the results of a lifelong love of all things creative, but the restaurant is also the result of Fillmoe, otherwise known by those who are not from the neighborhood as Fillmore, the neighborhood that raised me and gave me my swag, that taught me the importance of community while also instilling in me the importance of keeping it real and being true to myself.

Fillmoe is a neighborhood in northeast San Francisco about a dozen miles away from my restaurant, across the San Francisco–Oakland Bay Bridge. In the 1950s Fillmoe was known as the Harlem of the West, a place that was hella Black, with Black music, Black art, and Black food. Artists like Billie Holiday, John Coltrane, and Dizzy Gillespie all came through Fillmoe on their tours of the West Coast to perform for Black crowds at local spots like New Orleans Swing Club. Black nightclubs lined Fillmoe and Post streets, giving folks the chance to hang out with one another until the wee hours of the morning, listening to live music and having a drink. They were bring-ing the sounds of their homes on the East Coast or in the South with them to the West Coast, creating a community that resembled where they were from. If you really think about it, Fillmoe was where folks moved for jobs and opportunity, but underneath was homesick Black folks who built what they knew in their new spot.

When I was growing up, Fillmoe was a Black neighborhood and San Francisco felt like a Black city. Black businesses were everywhere in Fillmoe—Marcus Books, Mrs. Dewson's Hats, and the numerous bars

and restaurants that lined Fillmore Street, all of them Black-owned. My favorite record shop was called Mo Music for the People; it was owned by a Black entrepreneur who went by Showtime. Showtime is my mom's longtime friend, and I called him Uncle. Mo Music for the People was a hub for us growing up; they sold all the new CDs, incense, posters, and even clothes. My friends and I stopped by every Tuesday to buy new hip-hop albums. When I recorded my first album, I wanted to buy a fake Versace shirt from the store to wear on my album's cover photo, but I couldn't afford it because it cost $300. So, I went and talked to Showtime. He said if I swept up his shop for a couple weeks, he would let me have a shirt. That was that—we had a deal. I learned a lot from Showtime, and he set an example for many of us growing up.

Seeing Black people own their own spaces made us kids in the Fillmoe feel like we were surrounded by greatness. It made us believe that we were and could be great, too. It was inspiring. It also made the neighborhood feel like a big family. We all looked out for one another as we grew up.

When gentrification pushed Black people out of San Francisco, the change to Fillmoe was quick—so quick that it almost makes me forget how it used to be. A lot of Black people from San Francisco have moved to Oakland and other Bay Area cities. Walking through the neighborhood now, you can see remnants of what it used to be like, but a lot of it is gone. Oakland now feels like how Fillmoe used to: a Black mecca of the West, where we can still tell our stories and own our own spaces.

The Fillmoe had (and still has) its own swag that will always infuse everything that we do, and it inspires music from around the Bay. We have a lot of confidence and a lot of talent, and I carry that in myself and in my music. Our culture here has influenced music worldwide. R&B legends such as Tony! Toni! Toné! and En Vogue, and rap legends like Too $hort and E-40, are just a few of many iconic musicians from the Bay Area. Bay Area musical history and tradition has created and will create generations of talented musicians going forward.

I use music in the same way I use food—to express myself and tell my story. Music has always been one of my main loves, and I always knew I wanted to be a rapper. As a teenager, I wrote rhymes about hustling and being a player, hanging out at the park, and tagging buses. I sold mixtapes out of my school locker. Hip-hop informed my life at that point, taught me to keep it real with everything I did. Soon, I was recording my first album with Done Deal Records, with plans to go nationwide. I felt like I was doing something really big. My mom was tripping; she didn't want me to sign a contract, miss school, or drop out. But I still went to the recording studio three days a week after school to record my music. My love of making music emerged during those times.

When I was eighteen and old enough to sign my own contracts, I started putting out my music officially. I was in a group called Fully Loaded with Big Rich and Bailey, two West Coast rap legends. Being in the studio with them and legends like Messy Marv, one the most influential gangsta rappers in the Bay Area, showed me how to keep up my skills. One time I was in the studio with the Fully Loaded crew and Messy Marv. We had been chilling, so everyone was lit. Marv was slumped over in his chair dead asleep. We had to shake him awake to go into the booth to record his verse. He jumped up and did the most fire verse I've ever heard in my life. We were like, "Man, this boy is crazy." Seeing rappers like San Quinn also helped shape me and taught me to get up, knock out what I'm doing, and bring style to everything I do. Just like you can tell when a rapper is from Harlem from the sound, you can tell when a rapper is from Fillmoe.

Even to this day, my food—everything I do—is hip-hop. Remixing dishes, making them vegan, and blending influences to make a new recipe requires me to be creative in the kitchen just like I'm creative on the mic. When I'm in the kitchen, I'm expressing myself. Just as those music skills rubbed off on me, learning from my family and being in the Bay really, *really* rubbed off on me in terms of food. With food and music, the Bay is a mixture of influences coming together to create something unique.

Almost five years ago, I decided to go vegan because I wanted to be healthier. I had caught the flu, and it felt like it wasn't going any-where. I wasn't getting better, and I was also scared because people were dying from pneumonia. A friend of a friend—another parent who had a child in my daughter's soccer group—died from it. After that I started juicing and drinking hella ginger shots. Then I decided I didn't want to eat meat anymore, and after that I cut out dairy. I stopped cold turkey to kick the flu, basically, and so I could be health-ier to invest in my future. I wanted to be around for my kids and their kids. When I cut out meat, I found that I had more energy, and my emotional state was better, too. I was more positive. It was enough to encourage me to make a long-term change. But I had no idea that eating this way would lead me down a whole different career path. Today I feel better than ever.

But being vegan, I missed the things that I grew up eating, like soul food and barbecue. I *really* love barbecue. It's one of my favorite things to eat and I hated the idea of never having it again. When I was growing up, my uncle "Bobby Joe" from Texas showed me how to make barbecue at home because, as he put it, "San Francisco don't know nothing about no barbecue." Years after he passed, when I decided to open a restaurant I thought, "Why don't I try making

barbecue without meat? I'm gonna show him and everyone else how we make this barbecue vegan style." I didn't know exactly where to begin, but I just started with what I knew: macaroni and cheese, fried chicken, and brisket. I started simple, just smoking and grilling plant-based proteins at home, making sauces, and testing recipes until they started to feel right. I looked for vegan substitutes, especially for vegan proteins that hit just like the originals, and thought long and hard about how I could make substitutions that would keep the same flavor, the same soul, just without the meat.

When I see the line at the shop every day, I see all of that coming together: history and my specific story of growing up in this area, putting it all on the plate for my community to taste. And it speaks to my current life as a vegan and wanting to offer healthy alternatives to the neighborhood. The food that I'm making is vegan, but it's also soul food and barbecue, two types of food that my family made that tie me back to my Texas and Louisiana roots. My family came to the Bay from those areas and brought their family recipes with them. A lot of the food that I make is based on favorite comfort food dishes that most vegans think they'll never get to eat again. I love seeing people smile when they realize they can eat something they haven't had in a long time. Even nonvegans are surprised at the fact that what they're eating has so much flavor without meat. When Southern nonvegans tell me I make good soul food, it's the best compliment I can ever get.

Vegan Mob comprises all the things that inspire me: the love of my city, the love of hip-hop, and of course, the love of good-ass food. It's rebellious, it's gritty, it's real. Food and hip-hop are my passions, and I want to share them with my community and the world. I see Vegan Mob as a way to continue to tell stories of Black people in the Bay. I want the future to be like the past of the Fillmoe. I want to see more Black businesses, more diversity in the types of businesses that get to open.

It's da mob.

VEGAN PANTRY

The vegan market is constantly changing, so I'm always testing and trying new products to see what's out there. There are OG brands such as Tofutti, Tofurkey, or Follow Your Heart, but newer, smaller companies are popping up with really interesting offerings that are inspired by meat products. Here are my favorite brands and products that show up in my recipes and on my menu.

Meat Substitutes

BeLeaf frozen shrimp — This is ideal when frying or coating, because the shrimp flavor and texture really come out that way.

Better Chew shredded chicken, chicken strips, or drumsticks — When coated and fried, it really gives you that chicken-like texture and taste.

Better Chew Original Shredded Steak — I use this because it actually reminds me of steak. It gives the right feel in things such as brisket and steak and eggs.

Beyond Meat Breakfast Sausage Patties — A good breakfast sausage goes a long way in things such as gravy and breakfast sandwiches. This is the first brand I found that makes breakfast sausage patties. There are more options for vegan breakfast patties on the market now but this one is soy-free and it tastes like the sausages I remember eating when I ate meat.

Beyond Meat Hot Italian or Sweet Italian Sausages — Dishes such as gumbo and baked beans wouldn't be the same without a little hint of meatiness.

Impossible Burger Patties — These give that salty, drool-worthy bite you usually get when biting into a burger.

Impossible ground beef — This is my go-to for any time I'd usually use ground beef—think tacos, chili, meatloaf, spaghetti sauce, and more. It's the closest thing to a burger as far as vegan substitutes go. To me, no other brand has come as close to being like beef as Impossible.

Tofurky Deli Slices — This is perfect for any lunch sandwich, like turkey melts or clubs. Tofurkey is one of the original vegan brands and they've got the recipe down for making something taste like deli meat. They hold the title in my eyes—my daughter even likes it and she's picky as hell.

Lightlife hot dogs — For the right snap and chew, this is it. They taste just like meat hot dogs, reminiscent of ball parks and cookouts.

Tom Nguyen Con Soy-based Shrimp — This product is good for shrimp fried rice or soups where you aren't going to be dredging the shrimp in flour to fry up. It's meatier and holds up when introduced in a dish that has liquid. If you can't find this brand, you can use the BeLeaf brand mentioned above.

Umaro Bacon — Not all vegan bacon can get the job done, but this one crisps up just like the real thing. Umaro is a Black-owned company and they make their vegan bacon with nutritious red seaweed, so that's an added bonus.

Dairy Substitutes

Best Foods Vegan Dressing & Spread mayo — We all know that you can't make potato salad or a proper sandwich without some good mayo. You can't get any better than this. I don't know their secret, but I know that you can't tell the difference between this and non-vegan mayo.

Earth Balance butter — This is your all-purpose butter—from mashed potatoes to peach cobbler, it gives everything that silky, buttery goodness. Before I was even vegan I was using it to add flavor to my dishes.

Daiya Cheddar slices and shreds — The shreds melt in a custardy way that makes them perfect for chili, hot dog, and taco toppings. The slices turn out all smooth, which is exactly what you want for grilled cheese and jalapeño poppers.

Follow Your Heart Parmesan, Smoked Gouda, American, and Mozzarella Cheese — The best for lasagna, garlic bread, pasta, and quesadillas. The flavor of the gouda and parmesan is nutty, and the American and mozzarella cheese both melt really well.

Jell-O Vegan Vanilla Pudding Mix — Jell-O is a household name for a reason—the consistency of the pudding gives your banana pudding and coconut cream pies the right mouthfeel.

JUST Egg egg substitute — I can use this for basically any meal of the day—omelets, meatloaf, sweet potato pie, and more! It has a rich egg flavor and it looks like the real thing too.

Miyoko's Creamery cream cheese — Rich and creamy, this cashew-based spread is perfect for mixing with other cheeses in a lasagna or slathering straight on your bagel sandwich. There are so many cream cheeses on the market now, but I come back to this one because it's so flavorful and adds a great texture to whatever you're using it for.

Miyoko's Creamery Fresh Italian-style Mozzarella — This fresh mozzarella works on pizza or on a cheese plate. The texture is just like cow's milk–based mozzarella and it has a great melt.

Mocha Mix coffee creamer — This really does the trick to get the right creamy texture in Alfredo sauce or mashed potatoes. I haven't found another creamer that can add a level of creaminess without being too thick like this one does.

Ripple Unsweetened Original pea milk — It's super creamy and gives body to sauces, like my lemon sage parm and nacho cheese.

Ripple Unsweetened Plant-based Half & Half — The thickness of this half-and-half gets waffle batter to the right consistency. It's also unsweetened so you can use it in both sweet and savory recipes.

Ripple Heavy Cream — I like to use this heavy cream when I want a very rich taste in my clam chowder or pasta sauces. Ripple uses pea protein, which gives everything it's added to a thick, creamy texture. It's the unsung star in my Smackaroni and Cheese (page 38), giving the cheese sauce a great texture that works well with vegan cheddar.

Sprouts Oat Milk Whipped Topping or So Delicious CocoWhip — Sometimes I'm in the mood for more coconut flavor, so I use So Delicious. When I want to make something where I think coconut will overpower the rest, I choose the oat-based topping instead. I prefer the So Delicious CocoWhip because the texture is so smooth. I also love their ice cream.

Tofutti cream cheese — Thick and soy-based, this is the right call for dips and creamed veggies. It's versatile and texturally lends itself to mixing.

Tofutti sour cream — Everyone knows you must finish off your chili and loaded nachos with a dollop of sour cream, and this one has just the right amount of mellow tartness. It's the best vegan sour cream there is, because it isn't nut-based like a lot of other vegan sour creams on the market.

"FILLMOE MAY HAVE GIVEN ME MY SWAG, BUT MY GRANDMOTHER GAVE ME SOUL."

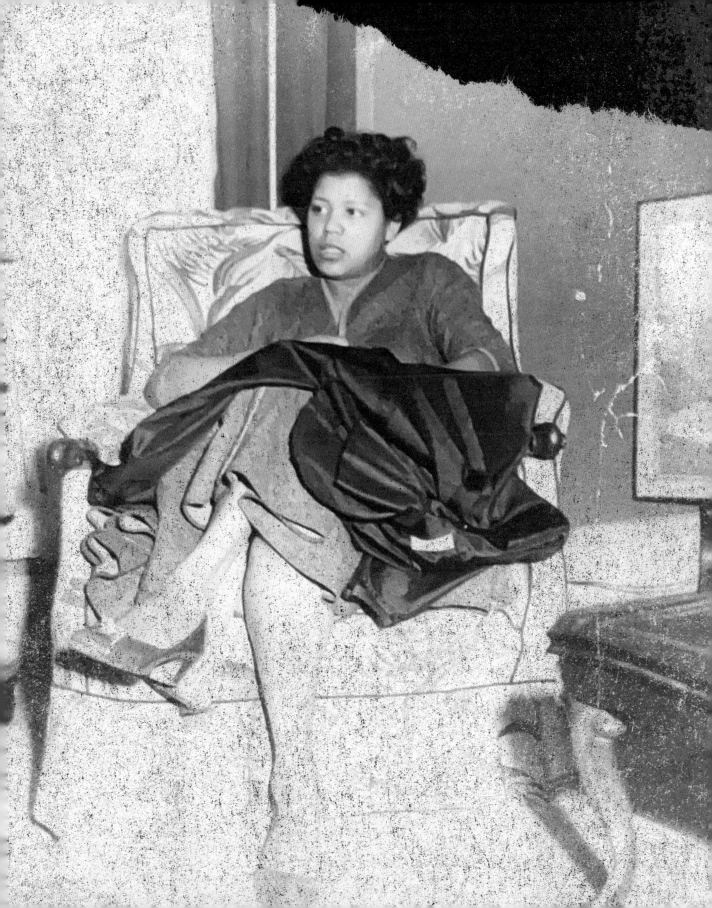

THE SOUL OF VEGAN MOB'S SOUL FOOD

There's two parts to good food: the way it's made (technique) and soul. When I think about why Vegan Mob is what it is, it's because of my family. I learned technique from my Uncle Bobby Joe, but I got a taste of the soul in soul food from my grandmother, Mattie Jackson, and my great Aunt Nanny. If you take a good look at Vegan Mob's menu, you'll see that I'm not only trying to make bomb-ass vegan food; I'm also telling a story. Specifically, I'm telling the story of the women in my family, especially my grandmother, who moved to the Bay from Texas and used her courage to make a life for herself and her family. In her kitchen, in a new place, she made the food she missed from home and passed that bit of culture on to her children and her grandchildren. The soul of Vegan Mob is the soul I inherited from my grandmother, that I tasted in the plates of food I ate in her house with my family.

Mattie Jackson was born in Texas in 1921, during the Great Depression, and moved to the Bay twenty years later when my grandfather got a job at the shipyard in San Francisco. She got her first job in the city after seeing a Cashier Wanted sign in a window. That may not sound like a big deal, but you need to remember this was 1940s San Francisco. Everyone thought she was crazy for applying, because she was Black. But she did it anyway and got the job because she was good at math and worked quickly, beating a white woman who had applied at the same time.

Getting that job showed her what was possible out West, and she decided to make it home for her family. As she put it, in Texas she would have never thought about applying for that job because the state was so segregated at the time. As a Black woman in the South, she couldn't reach all the things she wanted to do. But after she moved out West, she eventually started her own businesses, owning a record store in Fillmoe and a corner store on Potrero in the 1960s before getting a job as a seamstress at Ben Davis Clothing, a clothing manufacturer that opened in 1935 and is still in operation today in California. She moved to another job at Koret, a big-name women's clothing manufacturer, where she was told she "wouldn't last long." There she noticed the people she worked with, mostly other women, weren't getting paid fairly. My grandmother brought all the hourly workers together to strike for unpaid and missing wages, and it was successful. She and the workers were paid back wages by

the company, and the action put her in touch with the International Ladies' Garment Workers' Union. That experience shifted things for her, and after that she went on to work for labor rights all over the city and the state. She was vice president of the Commission on the Status of Women, commissioner for the Human Rights Commission, and president of the Board of Permit Appeals, making sure people got treated fairly wherever they were working. She was such a legend. Even when she retired from working, she still stayed busy and opened an antique store called En Vogue.

But before I knew about her work in labor rights, I knew she was my grandmother, and I thought the best food in the world came from her kitchen. Since Mattie was from Texas, she cooked all the Southern favorites that she remembered from home, like gumbo with white rice, baked sweet potatoes with butter, and macaroni and cheese. She could really throw down in the kitchen, and all of us grandkids loved it when she cooked. She loved cooking succotash, fried chicken, pork chops with gravy and grilled onions, mashed potatoes, meat loaf, baked barbecue ribs, and all types of stuff. I thought maybe I was biased, because it was my grandmother's cooking, but even when friends came over, they'd comment on how good the food was. I'm hella lucky, too, because my grandmother and my family taught me all the classic dishes that they made. I would ask if I could help and they always said yes.

When it was a holiday, my family went to my grandmother's house, but when it was time for barbecue, we went to Aunt Nanny's house because she did it the best. My grandmother covered the soul food, and Aunt Nanny handled the barbecue. Aunt Nanny was my grandmother's sister, so technically my great-aunt. Aunt Nanny was a real one. She had a guest house in the back of her house that she'd let people stay in and she drove a big-ass '78 Lincoln Continental. Later on, she got a new one, a '94 or something like that, but she stuck with the Continental because she liked the style. She was a boss. On holidays we had smoked brisket with barbecue sauce or ribs she made from scratch at her house in Berkeley. Back when Aunt Nanny was around Berkeley, there were Black and brown folks around. That's not the case anymore, unfortunately.

When I think about her house in East Bay, I think about the smell of smoke and charcoal. She had a big-ass smoker behind her house. It was huge and black and rusted in some spots because it was so old. If we got to her place early, we'd see her putting in mesquite wood, setting up to put links on there for a couple hours, or sometimes ribs or brisket. I remember her just talking about how good her brisket was, and she wouldn't share details of how to cook it, but she seemed to get joy out of cooking and providing good food for our pleasure. I think she liked it, not only because it gave her bragging rights, but because everyone would come over and there'd be music playing in the backyard, sodas chilling in a cooler for kids, and adults drinking beers among the fig trees in her yard. It made her happy to see us happy and enjoying the food that she put love into.

Her house just felt like an auntie's, you know? The couches were covered in plastic, there were candy jars everywhere (which was my favorite thing because I could always grab some). Her kitchen was old school—though it had a dishwasher, which was new technology at the time—and it was mostly beige with oakwood cabinets and an electric stove. She'd stand at those counters cooking side dishes, trimming green beans, and ripping collard greens. Down the hallway from the kitchen was a deep freezer where she kept leftovers and meat. I learned from her to keep things in your home either in a freezer or canned, as a way to survive and take care of myself. She taught me to be resourceful and to create meals by looking around and seeing what I already have. She made some good food, and her barbecue was on point.

I always felt like Aunt Nanny's favorite kid in the family. She may not have said it, but she spoiled me differently than the other kids—even if she didn't tell me, I knew. When I ran away from my house at age fourteen after a fight with my mom, I went to her place, and I lived with her for a month. She took me in, and I'm grateful for it.

Aunt Nanny died two years after that, when I was sixteen, at the age of seventy-six. She had been picking green beans—she called them snap peas because she would snap them—and she had a heart attack in that same kitchen where she'd made so many meals for her loved ones. That was my first real tragic loss right there. The first time I really cried, painfully hard. I still miss her.

I went by Aunt Nanny's house in Berkeley a couple of years ago, and a bunch of memories came to me. It looked the same. Two trees in front and a green lawn, a red covered path to the front door, beige siding on the house. I think about those memories and how much they influence me today at Vegan Mob, where I make vegan barbecue and soul food. I really learned the power of food from my grandmother and my great aunt, and I don't even know if they meant to be so impactful. They were just doing what they knew: making meals for family, making what they liked to cook and eat, making the dishes they remembered from when they were growing up.

When I was five years old, my Uncle Olin helped me learn how to cook. Olin lived at my grandma's house, in a studio apartment that was on the first floor. He was my grandmother's father's brother. My uncle was cool. He introduced me to my first love: breakfast. I don't know if he should have been letting me use the stove at five or six, but he let me make simple stuff like oatmeal, eggs, bacon, biscuits, and toast. He showed me how to let the butter melt in the skillet until it got hot enough to add the eggs. I watched Uncle Olin pull the biscuits (he always used the ones that came in a can) from the oven when they were golden brown, not too brown. To this day I still love those biscuits. It made me feel so good to cook something and have it come out delicious. It also helped me get comfortable with cooking and stepping to the stove to make myself a meal.

My uncle Bobby Joe showed me how to make barbecue. It was my favorite food back when I ate meat. I was too young to learn from Aunt Nanny, but when I became a young adult, Uncle Bobby Joe was around, so he taught me. He showed me that the secret is to start with a good base: season the meat well, and you'll ensure it has plenty of flavor once you cook it. His cooking had a strong flavor from garlic powder, onion powder, paprika, chili powder, and lots of salt. He also always told me to cook brisket long and slow. He used what he called buzzard juice to add moisture to his brisket while it was cooking on the barbecue. His buzzard juice was a mixture of garlic, light beer, and melted butter. He used it to sop his meat occasionally while it cooked for hours. That liquid added moisture and flavor to whatever came off his grill, like his chicken or ribs.

Uncle Bobby Joe also taught me how to make his famous green beans and collard greens. He showed me that those dishes produce a lot of water, so you don't have to add a bunch more to your veggies. He used salt pork in his greens for flavoring. His green beans were my favorite, though, because of the flavor from the bell peppers, onions, and garlic, which I call my Uncle Mobby's Green Beans (page 123). That made me love vegetables and always want to add them to my meals, even when I was still eating meat.

When I think about the start of Vegan Mob, I realize that those meals and learning to cook those dishes was really where it all started. They got me hooked on cooking and experimenting in the kitchen. I always loved to cook and think of it like my rapping: both are hella creative, and I feel my best when I'm doing them. Those two parts of my life have been how I understand the world around me. In high school and as a young man, I used music to talk about what was going on around me, but in the kitchen, I could use cooking to explore the influences in my neighborhood.

People think of "soul food" as one thing, but there are a lot of different interpretations that all fall under the umbrella of soul food. When I started making music and touring the country, I always checked out soul food spots. It was much easier then because I wasn't vegan. When I went to New York, I visited Sylvia's, and the fried chicken tasted just like back home. In Atlanta, my friend took me to a bomb takeout spot for smothered pork chops, macaroni and cheese, and greens. It was hella good. In Kansas City, Missouri, I went to a place called Niecy's and had a similar meal: macaroni and cheese and fried chicken wings that were really good. The flavor profiles were the same: salty, creamy, crispy, earthy, and sometimes sweet. The soul was the same, but the ingredients were switched up a bit. I think that's what happens in California, too. In Cali, Black folks are from all over—Texas, Arkansas, Mississippi, Alabama, Georgia, you name it—so the soul food here is a product of those roots plus the fresh produce that's available. I remember the first time I had gumbo at my dad's mother's house. They put oysters in their gumbo, and it seemed odd to me, but that's how they make it in Louisiana. The other side of my family is from Texas, so their gumbo is different, made with a lighter roux and less seafood. But both versions were served with fried okra to add crunch to the finished dish. Seeing the similarities and differences among different types of soul food helped me start to put together how the food I ate with my family came to California. It gave me roots.

When I decided to go vegan, I missed the Southern food that my family made. I knew I had to figure out how to cook it for myself with no eggs, no cheese, no butter, and no milk. It was tough, but I kept my grandmother in mind. She had to figure out how to use California ingredients to make the dishes she remembered from back home in Texas, so I kept that mentality while I worked. I looked at what I had access to and started testing and experimenting until I hit the right taste. I found vegan recipes that I liked on the internet and remixed them, adding spice, smoke, and sauces until they tasted like what I remembered from my own family's table.

One of my favorite creations is my barbecue sauce, which at first I called "Mattie's Magic" before I renamed it Mob Sauce (page 147). When I went vegan, I had to make my own version of plant-based barbecue, and I knew I wanted to come up with my own sauce. I tried a bunch of vegan recipes I found out there, but nothing tasted right. So I played around. I put a ton of work into the sauce, testing different ingredients I could find around the neighborhood. I tried just about every condiment out there, in different combinations, to try to get it just right. It had to have sweetness, tanginess, and smoke all in balance, just like my favorite barbecue sauces from back in the day. I also mixed in elements from different cuisines, adding lemon juice, and soy sauce, and sake. Every batch got me closer to what I wanted it to taste like, and when it finally came together, I knew immediately. It was like magic, so that's what I called it: Mattie's Magic.

Right before my grandmother passed away in 2009, I stood by her bedside in the hospital, holding back tears. I promised her that I'd take care of our family and make sure we're good. She couldn't speak, but she nodded as she listened to me and squeezed my hand as she held it in her palm. At that time in my life, I was in hell, drinking and smoking every day trying to feel better for a little while before I'd be depressed again. Losing my grandmother made me get my shit together and start pursuing my dreams. I couldn't let her down.

I started my business wanting to make good on that promise to my grandma, and Mattie's Magic infuses that promise every day.

SMOKED VEGAN BRISKET

Growing up we had Texas barbecue, and everyone knows that in Texas barbecue there's always brisket. Brisket, links, and chicken were all my aunties and family talked about all the time. I was always hearing somebody say "We're gonna smoke some brisket." When I decided I wanted to make vegan barbecue, I put together spices I remembered using with meat, like salt, garlic powder, and onion powder. I used Better Chew brand steak because I liked it—it actually reminded me of steak. I was so happy to be able to come up with a vegan brisket, and people love it. This is definitely a Mob favorite. If you really want to get the soul of this dish, you'll want a smoker and wood chips. If you absolutely cannot figure that out, you can add a tablespoon of liquid smoke and mix it in with the vegan meat when you add the seasonings. I would highly encourage you to try and smoke it for real, though, to get the full experience.

1— Set up a smoker by putting the wood chips of your choice in the smoking basket and lighting them until they begin smoking steadily, but not in a way that overwhelms the smoker.

2— In a perforated pan, toss the vegan steak with the salt, garlic powder, black pepper, and onion powder until fully coated.

3— Smoke the brisket over low heat for 1 hour, until the shredded steak is smoky but not overpowering.

4— Transfer to a serving bowl, add the Mob Sauce, toss, and serve immediately.

MAKES 2 CUPS (SERVES 4)

2 (7-ounce) packages shredded vegan meat, preferably Better Chew Original Shredded Steak

1 tablespoon kosher salt

1 tablespoon garlic powder

1 tablespoon freshly ground black pepper

1 tablespoon onion powder

1 cup Mob Sauce (page 147)

SMACKARONI AND CHEESE

I grew up eating my grandma's macaroni and cheese. It had Velveeta, evaporated milk, sometimes a can of Campbell's Cheddar Cheese soup, and different kinds of cheese including cheddar. When I became vegan, grandma's mac and cheese was one of the things that was hardest for me to let go. I knew when veganizing this that it had to look and taste right. We call it Smackaroni for a reason. It's smackin'! (Aka: it's hella good.) It's creamier than most vegan macs because of the pea milk, which has an almost heavy cream–like consistency. I dice up slices of vegan cheddar along with the shreds to get pockets of cheese throughout. I like Daiya cheddar for this recipe because it melts perfectly. Make this for anyone who is skeptical about vegan comfort food.

SERVES 4 TO 6

1 (16-ounce) box elbow macaroni

1 stick (8 tablespoons) vegan butter, preferably Earth Balance

1 cup chopped green onions, white and green parts

2 tablespoons minced garlic

½ cup all-purpose flour

4 to 4½ cups pea milk, preferably Ripple

1 tablespoon kosher salt

2 (7-ounce) packs sliced vegan cheddar, preferably Daiya cheddar-style slices, coarsely chopped

1 (7-ounce) bag vegan cheddar shreds, preferably Daiya cheddar-style shreds

1— Preheat the oven to 350°F. Lightly grease a 9 by 13-inch baking pan. Bring a large pot of salted water to a boil.

2— Cook the macaroni in the boiling salted water according to the package instructions, until soft. Drain the pasta and set aside.

3— Melt the vegan butter in a large pot over medium heat. Add the green onions and garlic and sauté until softened, about 2 minutes. Add the flour and cook until flour is slightly toasted with a slightly nutty aroma, stirring with a whisk, about 3 minutes.

4— While whisking, pour in 4 cups of the pea milk and continue to stir until the sauce is thickened and smooth, about 5 minutes. Make sure to run the whisk along the edges of the pot to get all of the flour.

5— Turn the heat down to low and add the salt, vegan chopped cheddar, and vegan cheddar shreds. Cook for about 5 minutes, stirring occasionally, until most of the shredded cheese is melted. If the sauce is lumpy, add an additional ½ cup of pea milk and whisk until smooth.

6— Add the cooked macaroni and stir well to coat.

7— Pour the mixture into the greased baking pan. Cover with foil and bake for 20 minutes, or until the sauce is bubbly.

8— Let it cool for a few minutes and serve hot.

"GRATITUDE PROMOTES LIFE AND BOOSTS IMMUNITY. PRACTICING GRATITUDE EQUALS HAPPINESS."

CREAMY CAJUN POTATO SALAD

You know you gotta fuck with the potato salad! It's everyone's favorite side at the cookout. I like a really smooth potato salad with no lumps. But if you like it lumpy, that's up to you. I make this the day before I need it because it gets even better as it chills. But a couple hours in the fridge works, too.

1— In a large pot, cover the potatoes with cold water and add 2 tablespoons kosher salt. Over medium heat, bring to a boil and cook the potatoes until fork-tender, about 20 minutes. Drain and let cool slightly while you make the dressing.

2— In a large bowl, mix the vegan mayo, mustard, green onions, bell pepper, black pepper, Cajun seasoning, and a pinch of salt.

3— Add your slightly cooled (but still warm) potatoes and mix, mashing down the potatoes as you go to achieve your desired creaminess. Add salt to taste.

4— Cover the bowl and store in the fridge overnight, or for at least 2 hours before serving.

SERVES 4 TO 6

4 pounds red potatoes,
cut into 1-inch pieces

Kosher salt

¾ cup vegan mayonnaise, preferably
Best Foods Vegan Dressing & Spread

2 tablespoons yellow mustard

¼ cup chopped green onions,
white and green parts

¼ cup diced red bell pepper

1 teaspoon freshly ground
black pepper

1 teaspoon Cajun seasoning,
preferably Slap Ya Mama

VEGAN MOB GUMBO

This wouldn't be a soul food cookbook without a gumbo recipe. This recipe is special to me because it's one of the first things that got me hella juiced about opening Vegan Mob. I knew it was really good. This is an easy chop-and-drop recipe that gives big flavor. The addition of seaweed gives it that ocean-y taste that's in the background of every good gumbo. If you want it a little less spicy, cut back on the red pepper flakes.

SERVES 6 TO 8

½ cup olive oil

1 red bell pepper, seeded and chopped (about 1 cup)

1 green bell pepper, seeded and chopped (about 1 cup)

1 yellow onion, chopped (about 1 cup)

¾ cup diced celery (about 2 stalks)

2 tablespoons chopped garlic

1 tablespoon kosher salt

2 teaspoons dried red pepper flakes

1 teaspoon freshly ground black pepper

½ cup all-purpose flour

8 cups veggie broth

2 (14-ounce) packages vegan Italian-style sausage, hot or sweet

1 ounce (¾ cup) dry seaweed or nori, shredded

2 bay leaves

Cooked white rice for serving

Fried Okra for serving (page 45)

1 cup chopped green onions, white and green parts, for garnish

1— Heat the oil in a large pot over medium-high heat. Add the red and green peppers, onion, and celery, and sauté until softened, about 3 minutes.

2— Add the garlic, salt, pepper flakes, and black pepper, and sauté for another minute, just long enough to cook the garlic. Add the flour and cook until flour is slightly toasted and coating all the veggies, stirring often with a wooden spoon, about 2 minutes.

3— While stirring, pour in the veggie broth and continue to stir until the gumbo is smooth and all the flour is incorporated, being sure to scrape the bottom of the pot to get any flour that stuck.

4— Slice the vegan sausages into bite-size pieces and add them to the pot with the seaweed and bay leaves. Bring everything to a boil, then lower the heat to simmer.

5— Simmer the gumbo over low heat, partially covered, for 1 hour, until the veggies are soft, the sausage is cooked, and the gumbo has a smooth, velvety texture. If needed, continue to cook for 15 minutes and check the veggies again. Remove the bay leaves.

6— Serve hot over white rice with plenty of green onions on top and your favorite hot sauce on the side.

"PLEASE TAKE CARE OF YOUR HEALTH. EAT VEGETABLES, FRUITS, AND DRINK WATER. TAKE VITAMINS. EAT PLANT-BASED!"

FRIED OKRA

My grandmother used to always make fried okra, especially to serve with gumbo. Over time, I lost my taste for it. But all my followers and customers from Louisiana always ask, "Where the fried okra? It's not gumbo without the fried okra." So, here's a recipe for your fried okra. I ain't gon' lie, it's bussin'. Dip it in one of the Mob Sauces and go crazy or toss it on top of your bowl of Mob Gumbo (page 42).

1— In a medium bowl, whisk together the cornstarch, 1 tablespoon of the garlic powder, 1 tablespoon of the onion powder, and salt. Add in the vegan creamer and mix. Set aside.

2— To a separate bowl, add the cornmeal plus the remaining garlic powder, onion powder, and cayenne. Line a plate with paper towels.

3— Working in batches, add a third of the okra to the creamer mixture and let it marinate for 1 to 2 minutes.

4— While the okra is marinating, heat the oil in a heavy pot over medium heat until a sprinkle of cornmeal sizzles when dropped into the oil.

5— Using a slotted spoon and working in batches, transfer the okra from the creamer mixture to the cornmeal and toss to coat thoroughly.

6— Drop the coated okra into the oil and cook until golden brown all over, about 2 minutes.

7— With a slotted spoon, remove the fried okra from the oil and set aside to drain on the paper towel–lined plate. Sprinkle the fried okra with salt while it's still warm.

8— Repeat the coating and frying steps with the remaining battered okra.

9— Serve immediately with gumbo or as a side dish.

SERVES 6

⅓ cup cornstarch

2 tablespoons garlic powder

2 tablespoons onion powder

1 tablespoon kosher salt plus more for sprinkling

1 cup plant-based creamer

1 tablespoon cayenne pepper

½ cup fine ground cornmeal

1½ cups sliced fresh or frozen okra, preferably fresh

2 cups grapeseed oil for frying

ORIGINAL BRISKET BARBEQUITO

This right here is a Mob favorite. Get you a side of Mob Sauce and a Peach Agua Fresca (page 215) to wash it down. You'll be hooked on this one!

1 — Lay out the wraps on your work surface and add half the brisket, half the sauce, half the slaw, half the Smackaroni, and half the beans to each, keeping the fillings to the center of the wraps so they are easy to fold.

2 — Bring the left and right sides of the wraps toward the centers. Then, from the bottom of the wraps, roll upward.

3 — Cut each in half using a serrated knife and serve.

SERVES 2

2 (12-inch) spinach or tomato vegan wraps, warmed

1 cup Smoked Vegan Brisket (page 37)

½ cup Mob Sauce (page 147)

½ cup Tasha's Slaw (page 57)

½ cup Smackaroni and Cheese (page 38)

½ cup Mobba'Q Baked Beans (page 53)

MOBBY GARLIC BREAD

This was a treat my mom used to make. We just loved eating garlic bread with pasta or steak and vegetables. Now that I don't eat steak, I put it on the side of pasta. Match it up with any of the pastas in this book and add the G-Money Mob Salad (page 133) to make it a full meal.

1— Preheat the oven to 350°F.

2— In a medium saucepan, melt the vegan butter. Pour on each half of the loaf. Sprinkle each half with the garlic, parsley, vegan parmesan, and the Creole seasoning.

3— Put the loaf back together and wrap in aluminum foil. Place in oven on a sheet pan and bake for 20 minutes, or until fragrant.

4— Remove from the oven, unwrap the foil, and slice. Serve immediately.

SERVES 6 TO 8

1 large loaf sourdough bread, halved horizontally

2 sticks (16 tablespoons) vegan butter, preferably Earth Balance

½ cup finely chopped garlic

½ cup chopped fresh parsley

½ cup grated vegan parmesan, preferably Follow Your Heart

2 tablespoons Creole seasoning, preferably Tony Chachere's Original

MOB GRAVY

I created Mob Gravy around Thanksgiving time because I was missing my grandmother's smooth, buttery gravy that she served with dressing, pork chops, and fried chicken. When I first made it, it was missing a meat flavor, so I added some chopped-up vegan breakfast patties because I remembered my mom sometimes added sausage to her gravy. At the restaurant, we serve this with Soul Mob Rolls for dipping (but Cheeseburger Rolls on page 206 would be dope too). Serve this with rice, mashed potatoes, and Mobby Fried Chicken (page 50). At Thanksgiving this will definitely make you feel like you're having the real gravy.

1— In a large saucepan, heat the olive oil over medium heat until shimmering. Add the onion, carrot, celery, and vegan sausage and sauté until vegetables are tender and onion is translucent, about 3 minutes.

2— Add the flour and stir to coat the sausage and vegetables. Cook for 3 more minutes, or until the flour is toasted.

3— Add the water to the pot and stir, being sure to scrape up any flour that may have stuck to the bottom of the pan. Whisk the mixture until it comes together into a thin sauce, about 2 minutes. Cook to remove the flour taste, about 3 minutes. Add the veggie bouillon base and black pepper and whisk.

4— Cover the pot and let simmer over medium-low heat for 30 minutes, checking every 10 minutes or so to ensure the mixture isn't boiling, until the flavors have melded. Taste and adjust the seasonings, adding salt if needed. Serve immediately.

MAKES 5 CUPS

3 tablespoons olive oil

⅓ cup chopped yellow onion

⅓ cup diced carrot

⅓ cup diced celery

2 vegan breakfast sausage patties, preferably Beyond Meat, chopped

1 cup all-purpose flour

4 cups water

2 tablespoons vegetable bouillon paste, such as Better Than Bouillon Seasoned Vegetable Base

1 teaspoon freshly ground black pepper, plus more to taste

Kosher salt (optional)

MOBBY FRIED CHICKEN

There's nothing better than some good-ass fried chicken. At the restaurant, we serve these patties with Mob Sauce, but you could definitely make a bomb sandwich with them, too. I use plant-based Better Chew Shredded Chicken for this recipe. When it's coated and fried, it really gives you that chicken-like texture and taste. This recipe will work with any vegan chicken strips, though. Making these can get hella messy, but I promise you, it's smackin'. Enjoy with Mob Sauce (page 147) or build a po' boy with a French roll and Tasha's Slaw (page 57).

SERVES 4 TO 6

4 cups all-purpose flour

2 tablespoons garlic powder

2 tablespoons onion powder

1 tablespoon Cajun seasoning, preferably Slap Ya Mama

1 tablespoon seasoned salt, preferably Lawry's

1 teaspoon kosher salt, plus more as needed

½ teaspoon freshly ground black pepper

2 cups water

1 pound vegan chicken (shreds, strips, or drumsticks), preferably 2 (7-ounce) packages of Better Chew, thawed if frozen

Vegetable oil for frying

1 — In a large bowl, mix 3 cups of the flour, garlic powder, onion powder, Cajun seasoning, seasoned salt, kosher salt, and pepper. While whisking, add the water to the bowl until the batter comes together. It should resemble a thick cake batter with no lumps. On a separate plate, mix together the remaining 1 cup of flour and a pinch of salt.

2 — If using vegan chicken shreds, take a small handful (about ¼ cup) and lightly coat them in the batter until you can form a disk in between your palms. Place the disk on the plate with flour and gently coat. Transfer the battered disk to a separate plate and repeat with the remaining chicken shreds. Refrigerate until firm enough to handle, about 15 minutes. If using vegan strips or drumsticks, coat each piece in the batter, roll in flour, and set aside.

3 — Pour 3 inches of oil into a heavy skillet or Dutch oven. Heat the oil over medium high to 350°F, or when a little bit of batter slowly bubbles up when dropped into the pan. Line a plate with paper towels.

4 — Working in batches, slip the battered vegan chicken into the oil and cook for 4 to 5 minutes, until golden brown and crispy. Drumsticks will take a bit longer, about 6 minutes. Drain the chicken on the paper towel–lined plate and add a sprinkle of salt. Repeat with the remaining chicken.

5 — Serve immediately.

"STAY POSITIVE AND STAY AMAZING. TAKE THE GREAT OUT OF THE WORST. NEVER SEE THE WORST, SEE THE LESSON. APPROACH LIFE WITH LOVE AND ALWAYS PRACTICE GRATITUDE."

MOBBA'Q BAKED BEANS

I love making these barbecue baked beans, even though I never really make them unless it's a special time of the year. Usually it's a barbecue-type holiday in the summertime. I love cooking these for a while in the oven because they taste like candy when they're done. These beans go crazy. Even if you don't like beans, you're gonna love these.

1 — Preheat the oven to 350°F.

2 — In a large heavy pot or Dutch oven, heat the olive oil over medium heat until shimmering. Add the onion, garlic, and salt and sauté for 2 minutes, or until translucent. Add the beans, sauce, vegan sausages, brown sugar, and mustard. Stir to combine and bring to a simmer. Let cook for about 5 minutes.

3 — Cover and bake for 1 hour, then remove the lid. Bake for an additional 35 minutes, or until beans have caramelized on top.

4 — Remove from the oven and let cool, then serve.

MAKES 4 CUPS (SERVES 8)

2 tablespoons olive oil

½ cup chopped white onion

2 tablespoons chopped garlic

1 teaspoon kosher salt

2 (15-ounce) cans pinto beans, drained

2½ cups Mob Sauce (page 147)

2 vegan hot Italian sausages, sliced, preferably Beyond Meat

3 packed tablespoons light brown sugar

1 tablespoon yellow mustard

MOBBA'Q SPAGHETTI

In Fillmoe, there was a place on Divisadero that served spaghetti with a side of barbecue sauce. I loved it—it was sweet and tangy, and you got the flavor of the meat at the same time. When I was making spaghetti for Vegan Mob, I mixed our house barbecue sauce into the plain spaghetti sauce to see if it tasted the same and it did, so I kept it on the menu. This version is also inspired by my stepdad, who taught me how to make spaghetti sauce in the first place. This sauce is super versatile—use in Mob Lasagna (page 61) or a Sloppy Mo' (page 91). For this dish, be sure to serve with plenty of grated vegan parm.

SERVES 4 (MAKES 4 CUPS SAUCE)

SPAGHETTI SAUCE

1 teaspoon olive oil

1 (12-ounce) pack vegan ground meat, preferably Impossible ground beef

1 teaspoon kosher salt

1 teaspoon freshly ground black pepper

1 cup tomato sauce

1 cup red wine

1 tablespoon granulated sugar

2 tablespoons chopped garlic

½ cup chopped fresh parsley

1 bay leaf

1 cup Mob Sauce (page 147)

1 cup chopped white onion

TO SERVE

½ box (8 ounces) spaghetti or pasta in the shape of your choice

1 cup grated vegan parmesan, preferably Follow Your Heart

1— Make the spaghetti sauce: Heat the oil in a heavy pot or Dutch oven over medium heat until shimmering. Add the vegan ground beef, salt, and pepper and cook until browned, breaking up the lumps with a wooden spoon, about 5 minutes. Add the tomato sauce, red wine, sugar, garlic, parsley, bay leaf, Mob Sauce, and onion and stir. Cook for 30 minutes to allow the flavors to blend.

2— Turn the heat to low and simmer for another 15 minutes, until the vegan meat is tender.

3— While the sauce is simmering, cook the spaghetti in boiling salted water according to the package instructions, and drain.

4— Remove the bay leaf. Combine the spaghetti with the sauce and serve immediately topped with the vegan parm.

TASHA'S SLAW

When I was growing up, my favorite aunt, my Aunt Nanny, made her famous coleslaw for our Fourth of July picnics. She was a cool woman—tough and a hell of a cook. This recipe is my take on that slaw, a version that has been in the family a long time and is great as a side dish to vegan barbecue or on top of a po' boy sandwich. I don't usually like slaw, but this shit is fire. My cousin Tasha gave me the recipe, and I added my own twist with a few things, including cranberries instead of raisins.

1— In a small bowl, whisk together the lemon juice, black pepper, salt, and vegan mayo. Set aside.

2— In a large bowl, toss together the cabbage, carrots, cranberries, and red onion. Combine with the mayo dressing mixture and toss to coat thoroughly. This is a good time to grab gloves and get your hands in there to mix it up good.

3— Taste and adjust the salt, if needed. Serve alongside Smoked Vegan Brisket (page 37) or on top of a po' boy (page 98).

MAKES 4 CUPS (SERVES 8)

1 tablespoon fresh lemon juice

1 teaspoon freshly ground black pepper

1 teaspoon kosher salt, plus more if needed

3 tablespoons vegan mayonnaise

½ head green or white cabbage, thinly sliced (about 4 cups)

2 carrots, shredded on the medium side of a box grater or mandolin

½ cup dried cranberries

½ cup sliced red onion

MOBBY MEATLOAF

When I want to feel like being a kid again, I make meatloaf. This version is just like my grandmother's and mom's meatloaf, except plant-based. It has a ketchup crust and everything. Keep any leftovers and make sandwiches with Mob Sauce (page 147) and vegan cheese. Sheesh!

1— Preheat the oven to 350°F.

2— In a large bowl, mix together the vegan ground meat, vegan egg, breadcrumbs, onion, garlic powder, dried thyme, salt, and pepper until well combined.

3— In a separate bowl, mix together the tomato sauce and ketchup.

4— Add the meatloaf mixture to a 9 by 5-inch loaf pan and pour the tomato sauce mixture over the loaf.

5— Cover and bake for 30 minutes. Remove the cover and bake for an additional 10 minutes, until browned.

6— Let cool for 15 minutes before slicing. Cut into 1-inch slices and serve immediately, with additional ketchup as desired.

SERVES 4

2 (12-ounce) packages vegan ground meat, preferably Impossible ground beef

½ cup vegan egg substitute, preferably Just Egg

2 tablespoons panko breadcrumbs

1 cup chopped yellow onion

1 tablespoon garlic powder

1 teaspoon dried thyme

2 teaspoons kosher salt

2 teaspoons freshly ground black pepper

1 cup tomato sauce

½ cup ketchup, plus more for serving

MOB LASAGNA

This is another thing my mom frequently made for us for dinner. People talk about her lasagna and it's kind of her specialty. If you had asked me when I was a kid, I had no idea it was Italian—I thought it was just dinner. When she made it, I was happy. I was so blessed to be able to have a mother who cooked like that for us, and it makes me think about how I want to provide that for my daughter. It really stuck that food is love and my whole family uses food to show love, too. This is a perfect dish to serve as dinner with a salad or to bring over to a friend's get-together.

1— Bring a large pot of salted water to a boil. Cook the lasagna noodles according to the package instructions, making sure not to overcook. Drain well.

2— Preheat the oven to 400°F. Set aside ¾ cup of the spaghetti sauce.

3— Make the cheese mixture: Mix together the vegan cream cheese and mozzarella in a medium bowl. Set aside.

4— In a 9 by 13-inch baking pan, add a layer of sauce, then enough lasagna noodles to cover the bottom. Top with a layer of half the cheese mixture. Add the chopped mushrooms. Sprinkle with the salt and pepper. Add another layer of sauce, top with another layer of lasagna noodles and the remaining cheese mixture, reserving ¾ cup of sauce.

5— Pour the remaining ¾ cup of sauce to cover the lasagna and sprinkle the vegan mozzarella shreds on top.

6— Cover the lasagna with aluminum foil and bake for 30 minutes. Remove the foil and bake for an additional 10 minutes to brown the cheese.

7— Remove the lasagna from the oven and sprinkle with the parsley and vegan parmesan. Let cool for 10 minutes, then serve.

SERVES 6 TO 8

1 (16-ounce) box lasagna noodles

4 cups Mobba'Q Spaghetti Sauce (see recipe on page 54)

½ cup chopped mushrooms

1 teaspoon kosher salt

1 teaspoon freshly ground black pepper

1 cup vegan mozzarella shreds, preferably Follow Your Heart

CHEESE MIXTURE

2 (8-ounce) containers vegan cream cheese, preferably Miyoko's

1 (8-ounce) container vegan fresh mozzarella, preferably Miyoko's Italian-style, grated

TO SERVE

¼ cup vegan parmesan shreds, preferably Follow Your Heart

¼ cup chopped fresh parsley

MOB CHILI

Every Halloween, my grandmother used to make a big pot of chili with rice on the side and some saltines. It was tradition. My mom stopped making chili on Halloween; she says she wants to make healthier things now. But I'll be real—I miss that rich, smoky chili my grandmother would make. This vegan recipe is inspired by her original. I still eat it with saltines and rice.

1 — Heat the oil a heavy pot or Dutch oven over medium heat until shimmering. Add the vegan ground meat, chili powder, salt, and pepper. Cook, breaking up the meat with a wooden spoon, until browned, about 5 minutes.

2 — Add the tomato sauce, wine, sugar, garlic, beans, bay leaf, and onion and stir.

3 — Let cook over medium heat for 30 minutes. Turn the heat to low and let simmer for about another 15 minutes, until the beans have softened and flavors have melded together.

4 — Remove the bay leaf, taste, and adjust the seasoning. Serve hot over white rice and top with vegan cheddar.

MAKES 4 CUPS (SERVES 4)

1 teaspoon olive oil

1 (12-ounce) package vegan meat, preferably Impossible ground beef

3 tablespoons chili powder

1 teaspoon kosher salt

1 teaspoon freshly ground black pepper

1 cup tomato sauce

1 cup red wine

1 tablespoon granulated sugar

2 tablespoons chopped garlic

1 (15-ounce) can kidney beans, rinsed and drained

1 bay leaf

1 cup chopped white onion

4 cups cooked white rice for serving

1 cup vegan cheddar-style shreds, preferably Daiya, for serving

MOBBUCCINE

aka Fettuccine Alfredo

I love fettuccine Alfredo, and I missed it so much when I went vegan that I worked on a recipe. I looked up vegan parmesan cheese and bought some, mixed it with some vegan chardonnay and vegan creamer and boom: I had Alfredo sauce. When I can't find anything I like, I make my own like this shit right here. If you're like me, you're gonna want to get a baguette or some extra bread and dip it into the sauce.

1 — Boil the pasta in a large pot of salted water according to package instructions, until al dente. Drain well and set aside.

2 — In a large saucepan, melt the vegan butter over medium heat and add the soy creamer, garlic, Cajun seasoning, and half of the grated vegan parmesan. Let cook over medium heat for 10 minutes. Add the wine and cook for another 10 minutes, until the sauce is smooth and creamy.

3 — Toss in the noodles and the remaining half of the parmesan. Serve immediately.

SERVES 4

1 (16-ounce) box fettuccine

Kosher salt

½ stick (4 tablespoons) vegan butter, preferably Earth Balance

2 cups vegan coffee creamer, preferably Mocha Mix

½ cup chopped garlic

1 tablespoon Cajun seasoning, preferably Slap Ya Mama

1 cup grated vegan parmesan, preferably Follow Your Heart

½ cup Chardonnay or other dry white wine

TASTY SPANISH RED RICE

This is my take on Spanish rice, which can go with a gang of things. I like it paired with Mobby Four-Bean Chili (page 71). This is made with California Red Jasmine Rice, which you can order online, but you can also use white rice. It's really tasty and healthy at the same time. You can serve this with your tacos and some refried beans or in the Original Brisket Barbequito (page 46).

1— In a heavy pan with a lid or a Dutch oven, heat grapeseed oil over medium heat until shimmering, about 2 minutes.

2— Add the rice and stir with a wooden spoon, allowing the grains to toast. Continue cooking, stirring constantly, for up to 3 minutes, or until the grains are light tan in color and begin to smell nutty.

3— Add the garlic, cumin, garlic pepper seasoning, and salt and sauté for 45 seconds or until just fragrant.

4— Add the tomato sauce and vegetable broth and stir well to ensure no grains are stuck to the bottom of the pan.

5— Turn the heat to low and simmer for 15 minutes, stirring occasionally.

6— Cover the pan and continue simmering for an additional 15 to 20 minutes, or until the rice has absorbed all of the liquid.

7— Fluff the rice with a fork and serve immediately.

SERVES 2 TO 4

2 tablespoons grapeseed oil

1 cup California Red Jasmine Rice, or short-grain white rice

3 large cloves garlic, chopped

1 teaspoon ground cumin

1 teaspoon Lawry's garlic pepper seasoning

1 teaspoon kosher salt

1 cup tomato sauce

2 cups vegetable broth

CREAMY CREOLE MOB SPINACH

A lot of my recipes are influenced by what I used to eat when I wasn't vegan. This recipe is inspired by the creamed spinach I used to love at Boston Market. I would order it at lunch all the time in my early twenties when I worked at a Best Buy in Frisco. When I first went vegan and was trying out new dishes to make, this was at the top of my list. You can serve this as part of a Vegan Mob–style mafia plate with some classic fried shrimp (see the classic variation in the headnote on page 75) and some Garlic Mob Potatoes (page 68).

1— Bring a large pot of water to a boil and add the salt.

2— Add all of the spinach, using a spoon to push the leaves down so they cook evenly, and cook for 2 minutes, until the greens are tender. Drain well, allowing the spinach to sit in the colander for 2 minutes.

3— Move the greens to a large bowl and, while they are still hot, add the vegan butter and cream cheese. Mix until creamy, being sure to break up any lumps that form.

4— Taste, season with pepper, and adjust the salt, if necessary. Serve immediately.

SERVES 2

3 tablespoons kosher salt, plus more as needed

2 (8-ounce) bags fresh spinach

3 tablespoons vegan butter, preferably Earth Balance, cut into chunks

¼ cup vegan cream cheese, preferably Tofutti

Freshly ground black pepper

GARLIC MOB POTATOES

These garlic mashed potatoes are one of my favorite dishes to eat. You can pair the garlic mash with my momma's green beans and some Mobby Fried Chicken (page 50) with Alfredo sauce. This dish here gonna get you right every time.

1— Bring a large pot of salted water to a boil over medium heat.

2— Add the potatoes, return the water to a boil, and cook until the potatoes are soft, about 15 minutes. Drain the potatoes and immediately return to the pot.

3— Add the vegan butter, vegan cream, parsley, garlic, black pepper, and salt to taste. Stir to combine, mashing the potatoes as you mix.

4— Taste and adjust the seasonings. Serve immediately.

SERVES 4

1½ pounds red creamer potatoes

1 stick (8 tablespoons) vegan butter, preferably Earth Balance, cut into 1-inch cubes

½ cup vegan heavy cream, preferably Ripple or Mocha Mix

¼ cup chopped fresh parsley

3 tablespoons chopped garlic

1 tablespoon freshly ground black pepper, plus more as needed

Kosher salt

GRAMMA'S COUNTRY CREAMED CORN

My grandmother used to always make creamed corn, like every other week, letting it simmer for hours. You don't have to do that though to get the same buttery, sweet flavor. This is a really good side with rice, gravy, and a main vegan protein to enjoy on a weeknight dinner. Dress it with hot sauce and serve with Mobby Fried Chicken (page 50).

1— In a heavy pot or Dutch oven, heat the olive oil over medium heat until shimmering, about 2 minutes.

2— Add the onion and sauté for 6 to 7 minutes, until the onion is starting to turn golden brown. Add the flour and stir to coat the onion evenly. Sauté for 3 to 4 minutes, until the flour begins to toast. Add the water and whisk to incorporate. Add the corn, sugar, salt, pepper, and garlic and stir.

3— Cover the pot and let cook for 30 minutes, until the corn has broken down a little bit but is still distinguishable. Stir frequently to ensure the bottom is not scorching.

4— Taste and adjust the seasonings with salt and pepper. Serve immediately.

**MAKES 2 CUPS
(SERVES 4 AS SIDE DISH)**

2 tablespoons olive oil

½ medium yellow onion, finely diced

½ cup all-purpose flour

½ cup water

1 (8-ounce) can whole kernel corn with liquid

1 teaspoon granulated sugar

1 teaspoon kosher salt, plus more as needed

1 teaspoon freshly ground black pepper, plus more as needed

2 medium garlic cloves, minced

MOBBY FOUR-BEAN CHILI

This is a healthier version of the chili that my family would make. I came up with this recipe when I was fasting and thinking about how I could make some of the vegan dishes I like to eat healthier, without the fake meat. This is about highlighting vegetables, and you don't necessarily need the plant-based meat substitutes to make something delicious.

MAKES 4 QUARTS (SERVES 8 TO 10)

1 — Combine the pinto beans, kidney beans, black beans, cannellini beans, zucchini, summer squash, red onion, white onion, garlic, tomato sauce, broth, chili powder, salt, and dried chipotle in a heavy stockpot or large Dutch oven over medium heat. Stir to make sure the ingredients are well mixed.

2 — Cook, stirring occasionally, until steam begins to rise from the pot and the ingredients are hot, about 10 minutes. Cover and let cook for 30 minutes.

3 — Taste and adjust the seasonings with more salt or chili powder.

4 — To serve, ladle the chili into bowls and add rice, vegan cheese shreds, diced tomato, vegan sour cream, and green onion. Serve with tortilla chips on the side.

1 (15-ounce) can pinto beans, rinsed and drained

1 (15-ounce) can kidney beans, rinsed and drained

1 (15-ounce) can black beans, rinsed and drained

1 (15-ounce) can cannellini beans, rinsed and drained

1 medium zucchini, diced

1 medium summer squash, diced

1 medium red onion, diced

1 medium white onion, diced

2 large garlic cloves, thinly sliced

2 (15-ounce) cans tomato sauce

1 cup vegetable broth

¼ cup chili powder, plus more as needed

2 tablespoons kosher salt, plus more as needed

1 dried chipotle pepper

TO SERVE

Tasty Spanish Red Rice (page 65)

Mexican-style vegan cheese shreds, preferably Daiya Mexican 4 Cheeze Style Blend

1 large tomato, diced

Vegan sour cream, preferably Tofutti

1 bunch green onions, white and green parts, diced

Tortilla chips for serving

GRAMMA'S COUNTRY CANDIED YAMS

It's not Thanksgiving or Christmas if there aren't candied yams on the table in my family. My grandmother always made candied yams, especially around the holidays, so I came up with the recipe just watching her cook for our family. I've blessed y'all with her exact recipe (she uses dairy butter though), and I may be in trouble with my family for sharing it.

1— Preheat the oven to 350°F.

2— In a medium baking pan, layer the sweet potatoes with cubes of the vegan butter, being sure to evenly distribute the butter among the sweet potatoes. Sprinkle the nutmeg, cinnamon, sugar, and salt over the cubes.

3— Cover the dish with aluminum foil and bake for 30 minutes, or until the sweet potatoes are soft when tested with the tip of a knife. Toss the mixture gently but thoroughly, making sure that all the pieces are coated in the syrup. It's okay if some of the chunks break up.

4— Return to the oven and bake, uncovered, for an additional 15 minutes to create a crust on top of the yams.

5— Let cool slightly, then serve.

SERVES 4

2 pounds sweet potatoes, peeled and cut into 1-inch chunks

½ stick (4 tablespoons) vegan butter, preferably Earth Balance, cut into 1-inch cubes

1 teaspoon ground nutmeg

1 teaspoon ground cinnamon

¾ cup granulated sugar

1 teaspoon kosher salt

RAGIN' CAJUN FRIED SHRIMP

Necessity breeds invention. Two hours before we opened Vegan Mob, I had some defrosted vegan shrimp that I didn't know what to do with, so I threw them in some seasoned flour and deep-fried them. They tasted fire, so I added them to the menu and people loved them. It was an accident, but it worked out for the best. If you want, make these barbecue-style instead by tossing the fried shrimp in Mob Sauce (page 147), or do Buffalo-style by tossing in Mobbin'-Ass Buffalo Sauce (page 146). For classic fried shrimp—used in recipes all over this book—you can just leave out (or reduce the amount of) Creole seasoning. Serve with good-ass homemade fries.

1— Whisk together the flour, Creole seasoning, salt, and pepper in a large bowl.

2— Add the water in a steady stream while whisking until a batter forms. It should resemble a cake batter with few lumps.

3— Put the panko onto a plate and set aside.

4— In batches of six, dip the vegan shrimp into the wet batter and remove, shaking off excess batter. Set on the plate of panko breadcrumbs. Using your dry hand, toss the shrimp in the panko to coat all over and create a crust. When one batch of shrimp is coated, place on a sheet pan in a single layer. Continue working in batches until all the shrimp are coated.

5— Freeze the shrimp on the sheet pan for at least 3 hours until firm, or overnight.

6— When you are ready to cook, in a heavy pot or Dutch oven heat 3 inches of the oil until the temperature reaches 350°F, or until a pinch of flour sizzles when dropped in the oil. Line a plate with paper towels.

7— Fry the shrimp six at time, until they are golden brown all over, about 2½ minutes.

8— Remove from the oil and drain on the paper towel–lined plate. Repeat with the remaining shrimp. Serve immediately.

SERVES 4

1 cup all-purpose flour

2 tablespoons Creole seasoning, preferably Tony Chachere's Original

1 teaspoon kosher salt

1 teaspoon freshly ground black pepper

1 cup water

1½ cups panko breadcrumbs

2 (10-ounce) bag frozen vegan shrimp, preferably BeLeaf, defrosted

Vegetable oil for frying

"I TRY TO THINK LIKE A SCIENTIST. I START WITH AN END GOAL IN MIND

AND THINK ABOUT HOW TO GET THERE BY TREATING VEGAN INGREDIENTS DIFFERENTLY."

Elements of Vegan Comfort Food

In 2019, I got invited to a party my friend Bailey was throwing for his kid's birthday. I had become vegan about two years before and had been testing recipes, cooking vegan soul food for my family, so I thought this would be the perfect time to give Bailey a taste of what I had been working on. I got up early that day to make a big pan of vegan macaroni and cheese and put it together. I mixed cooked macaroni noodles with vegan cheese sauce and baked it in a big aluminum pan. When I pulled it out of the oven my heart sank: it was still pale, and the vegan butter I had used in the cheese sauce had broken. It tasted good, but I wanted it to look like a standard nonvegan macaroni and cheese, with a creamy sauce and golden color. I wanted people to try it and then be surprised when I told them it was vegan. This big pan of noodles and broken sauce looked off. But I was running out of time, so I packed it up and headed to the party. People liked it, but I was disappointed with how it came out.

After the party, Bailey (who I had also been in a rap group with) gave me some simple but honest feedback: "It's cool, but it could be better." That was all he needed to say. I thanked him and got back into the kitchen the next day, testing out different types of vegan milks, cheeses, and butters to find out which one made the creamiest sauce. That testing led me to the current recipe for Smackaroni and Cheese (page 38), one of Vegan Mob's best sellers.

All of the dishes on the Vegan Mob menu came from putting in work in my kitchen, making and testing vegan versions of dishes until they came out just right. Trial and error and lots of mistakes led me to finding the best way to create vegan soul food, in a way that pays tribute to the original while using vegan products. Those early mistakes were lessons that let me know how to make vegan recipes better. Plant-based products are hella adaptable, but the finished product often doesn't match up to a meat-based option because people don't apply the same principles that they would to meat dishes. Either a vegan dish looks bad and tastes good, or it looks good and tastes bad, or it has no flavor. I wanted Vegan Mob to be the opposite, where the food looks good and tastes just as dope.

Another experiment that paid off was my Cheeseburger Rolls (page 206). Before I got into the kitchen, I tried to picture them first: spring roll–shaped, filled with ground meat and melted cheese like you'd expect, but made with plant-based ingredients. The first time I made them I used lumpia wrappers, and they came out too small and greasy. They looked bad. For the next batch, I used a bigger wrapper and was extra careful to make sure they were tight and uniform. The presentation was on point, and they tasted good, too. I just had to keep playing with the recipe, and I eventually got to a dish that was good enough to put on the menu—and in this book. P.S.: Shout out to my sister, who told me to try making Cheeseburger Rolls in the first place.

My stepdad gave me this advice: cooking is a science. And I try to think like a scientist. I start with an end goal in mind and wonder how to get there by treating vegan ingredients differently. Lately, I've been playing with mimicking the texture of braised meats, soaking soy proteins so they cook and fall apart in the same way that tender braised and stewed oxtails do. I had to teach myself and do a ton of research—plus rely on my memory of meat—to create the dishes I wanted to make. I don't even think I'm doing anything that special; I'm just doing what I was doing before but with plant-based options instead of with meat.

In your own kitchen you can do the same thing. Learning to make main dishes such as vegan barbecue brisket, ribs, or fried shrimp means you can use those principles to freestyle and create great meals at home with your family and friends. I come up with new things to sell at the shop when I get hungry. I was at the restaurant and thought about a deep-fried, cheesy sandwich and worked with my team to create it. My manager at the time came up with battering it to keep it together and I added green onions to the cheese for flavor. I wanted a tomato sauce for dipping and thought the spaghetti sauce would work and it did. Boom: we had a new dish for the menu. Sometimes those are the best dishes, where you're not really tripping, you're just being creative. Sometimes it's a memory, or a suggestion from a customer or employee, or I might see something online that looks good but it's not vegan. Cooking flows better when you're not forcing it. Your stomach is coming up with that idea, and your stomach never lies. It'll always lead you to something that tastes good.

PUTTING DISHES TOGETHER

People think vegan food can't be satisfying, but I think it can be if you plan right. Just as you might pair a meat dish with sides that you're passing around the table, you can do the same thing with vegan comfort food and vegan barbecue. To plan out a meal, I just go back to things that I grew up eating that felt traditional. If you were going to a barbecue, you would have your smoked meat, macaroni and cheese, collard greens, and potato salad, and you dig in. Just because it's vegan doesn't mean you can't hit that same feeling. People can't believe my versions are vegan, and even nonvegans love them because the dishes taste great and they're familiar.

When you're in your kitchen, instead of thinking about one dish at a time, think about pairing things together. Create a spread of different dishes that have different flavors, different textures, and even different temperatures to create a full meal.

MANIPULATING VEGAN PROTEINS

I want Vegan Mob to be the gateway to people eating more vegan food, so I start with dishes that people are familiar with and think about how to make them using vegan ingredients. You can meet people where they are with vegan soul food, and say to them, "If you want a burger, you can still have that," or "If you want macaroni and cheese, you can still have that." There are definitely ways to highlight vegetables with salads and raw vegan dishes and stuff like that, and there's nothing wrong with that, but I feel like this is me meeting people with tastes they know. Learning how to make vegan proteins taste similar to meat products is a skill I've had to develop.

When you think about using vegan proteins to be creative with dishes you already know, you can really bring dishes you remember from your nonvegan days to what you eat now. The most rewarding feeling I get is when Black people recognize what I'm trying to do and see the food they grew up eating being prepared in a new way. Some people do too much and want a literal interpretation, but you've got to use your imagination or you're not going to be able to create.

Mostly you want to think about how meat is used to flavor certain dishes and think about what vegan proteins you can use to mimic that flavor. My family loves using salt pork and bacon to flavor greens and other dishes, so I started to use vegan bacon bits to create a smokiness and bring a pork flavor to my greens and my gumbo.

Today most health food stores will have a lot of different vegan proteins available. Most plant-based proteins are available online, too, and you can order them. You can find bigger brands, such as Beyond Meat and Impossible, in your stores and online. I don't make the protein myself (I really want to in the future), but I can add texture with breading or by cooking it. Sometimes the plant-based substitute I'm working with doesn't even match what I'm trying to mimic. For example, to make vegan Buffalo chicken using fried mushrooms (page 204) so that it tastes like real Buffalo chicken wings, I have to slice and prep oyster mushrooms and marinate them in a sauce so that their texture and flavor mimic what actual wings feel and taste like. I remember the flavors and textures from traditional Buffalo wings, and I'm trying to satisfy both people who are familiar with the original dish and people who have never had meat wings before in their life.

I encourage people to play around, and if they don't have a natural scientific ability, then look up what will make things softer or juicier or creamier. That's how anything starts—with curiosity. Once you start to explore, you can acquire the knowledge and make all of the vegan dishes you want. As you cook more, your creative side will grow, and making vegan foods will become second nature.

VEGAN BARBECUE

People seem to think that when you're using vegan proteins, you don't need to follow the same rules of barbecue, and that's just not true. When you're making vegan barbecue, it requires using and mastering the same five elements as making barbecued meat.

Heat

When you apply heat to vegan protein, you have to be careful because too much heat will make it fall apart, and not enough won't allow it to cook and have the right texture. Being careful about how high your heat is on your grill and how long you're leaving your protein there is key. I typically stick to a temperature of about 200°F, and I use the thermometer on my smoker to make sure it's staying there. If you have a thermometer, you can use that, but if you don't, look at the charcoal. A good rule of thumb is that when the lit charcoals turn white, it's at a good temperature. Then you can put your soaked wood chips on top of the charcoal to create some smoke. And don't forget to leave the vent open so your fire can breathe a little bit.

Smoke

The first time I made vegan barbecue I had no idea how it would go—I was just trying it, seeing if I treated vegan sausages and brisket like meat how it would come out. I left them on the smoker too long and they were too smoky, to the point where you couldn't taste any other flavor. As I've developed other recipes, I've realized that smoke is a crucial way to create a dish that tastes like meat barbecue. Setting up your smoker with quality wood chips is key and you can use applewood chips, hickory chips, any wood that gives it the flavor you're looking for. You can even soak the wood chips in Jack Daniel's or another whiskey to impart the flavor—it's not super noticeable, but you get a hint of it.

You can play with using different wood smoke on different vegan proteins until you get something you like. I like hickory wood a lot for my brisket and sausages, but I played around with a lot of woods, like pecan, apple, and maple.

You know your smoker or grill is set up right for smoking when the pit is around 200°F and hazy when you open it, not too smoky. It shouldn't have a thick cloud of smoke. If it's too smoky, close the vent a little bit so there's less oxygen. If you don't have enough, leave the vent open so it can get some oxygen. It should smell pleasant, like delicious wood burning, not like gas. If it smells like gas, it's too hot and you should start over or your barbecue will have a burnt taste.

SEASONING AND FLAVOR

In the Bay, when something is really good, we say it's "smackin'." You know right away when something is hitting in terms of flavor. Testing your vegan barbecue and making sure the flavors are on point is so important. People think you can just cover up some bad barbecue with barbecue sauce, but that won't hide vegan meat that doesn't taste good on its own. You wouldn't put a piece of meat on the grill with no seasoning and expect it to come out good, so don't expect vegan meat to be different. In my kitchen I always have salt, black pepper, garlic powder, and Creole seasoning on hand to make my vegan proteins taste like meat and make sure they have hella flavor. You can play around with spices you already use, like cumin, paprika, different salts like pink Himalayan or even flavored salts, and other spices to find a mix you like.

You should also make sure your grill is seasoned. If you haven't used it before, get it hot and grill some onions or some bell peppers or some vegetables to start to build a crust of flavor on the grates. It'll give you that much more flavor when you're ready to make some barbecue.

TIME

Certain proteins are going to take less time to cook than others. Sautéing vegan ground beef for example will not take as long as vegan chicken fingers, which need to be baked or fried until they're the right temperature and cooked through. The same is true in the smoker when dealing with different proteins. With sausages I'm cooking and imparting smoke at the same time, so they take a little less time than brisket, where I'm using smoke and heat to impart flavor and reach a desired texture. It's trial and error, but I usually smoke sausages for less than an hour and brisket for about two.

By the way, that story about the friend who threw the birthday party where I brought macaroni for has a happy ending: when I finally got the recipe right for the Smackaroni, I brought him some of the new batch. He tasted it and said it was going crazy! I knew I had finally found a recipe that worked.

MOB LINK SANDWICH

In San Francisco at the 49ers games, you always see these nice-looking bratwurst and Italian sausage sandwiches. If I'm being honest, I miss those sandwiches. I wanted to make a sandwich that reminded me of going to the games, so I came up with this recipe. This is perfect to make when you're about to sit down and watch your team play.

1— In a large sauté pan, heat the olive oil over medium heat until shimmering. Add the peppers and salt and sauté for 4 minutes, until the peppers are soft. Set aside.

2— Toast the vegan hot dog buns and set aside.

3— Add the vegan sausages to the pan, or place on a grill if using, and cook, moving frequently until the internal temperature reaches 165°F.

4— Divide the peppers among the hot dog buns and top each with a sausage. Serve alongside your favorite condiments.

SERVES 4

2 tablespoons olive oil

1 red bell pepper, seeded and sliced

1 yellow bell pepper, seeded and sliced

1 green bell pepper, seeded and sliced

1 teaspoon kosher salt

4 vegan hot dog buns

1 (4-link) package sweet Italian sausage, preferably Beyond Meat

Condiments for serving

SLOPPY MO' ON TEXAS TOAST

This sandwich is another childhood favorite of mine that has become a favorite of my daughter as well. She keeps asking me when I'm going to make her more sloppy joes. This is a great way to use up extra spaghetti sauce or make a quick dinner on the fly.

1— Preheat the oven broiler to high.

2— In a small bowl, mix the vegan butter and minced garlic until well combined. Coat each side of the toast with some of the butter, spreading until it covers most of the toast. Place on sheet pan and set underneath the broiler. Let brown for about 2 minutes per side, until fragrant and bubbling.

3— While the bread is still warm, top two pieces with slices with vegan cheddar-style cheese. Set aside.

4— Heat the spaghetti sauce in a small saucepan or in the microwave until warm.

5— Place one cheese-covered slice and one uncovered slice on each plate.

6— Pour ½ cup of the warmed spaghetti sauce on top of the unbuttered toast. Top with the other toast, cheese facing the sauce. Repeat with remaining toasts. Garnish with vegan parmesan. Serve immediately.

SERVES 2

3 tablespoons vegan butter, preferably Earth Balance, at room temperature

2 teaspoons minced garlic

4 slices Texas Toast–style thick-sliced bread or your favorite vegan bread

2 slices vegan cheddar-style cheese, preferably Daiya

1 cup Mobba'Q Spaghetti sauce (page 54)

Grated vegan parmesan, preferably Follow Your Heart, for garnishing

CHICKEN 'N' WAFFLE BUSSDOWNS

My wife loves chicken and waffles. We used to go to a spot in San Francisco that's no longer around and get her a plate of chicken and waffles because it reminded her of her dad (he's from LA and loved Roscoe's). I wanted to come up with something that would remind her of her favorite dish. This is a pretty involved recipe; maybe something you would do on a weekend when you have plenty of time. Round up your family and have them help you.

SERVES 6

WAFFLES

1 cup vegan egg substitute, preferably Just Egg

2 cups all-purpose flour

1¾ cups unsweetened plant-based half-and-half for cooking, preferably Ripple

½ cup vegetable oil

1 tablespoon ultrafine granulated sugar, such as White Satin

4 teaspoons baking powder

¼ teaspoon kosher salt

½ teaspoon pure vanilla extract

Nonstick cooking spray

CHICKEN

2 cups all-purpose flour

1 tablespoon Cajun seasoning, preferably Slap Ya Mama

2 cups Mobbin'-Ass Buffalo Sauce (page 146)

Vegetable oil for frying

1 (8-ounce) package frozen vegan fried chicken, preferably Better Chew Fried Chicken, thawed

Pure maple syrup, warmed, for serving

1— Preheat the waffle iron. Preheat the oven to 200°F.

2— Make the waffles: In a large mixing bowl, beat the egg substitute and add in the flour, vegan half-and-half, vegetable oil, sugar, baking powder, salt, and vanilla. Mix until smooth.

3— Spray the preheated waffle iron with nonstick cooking spray and pour about 1 cup of the batter into the hot waffle iron. Cook until golden brown, about 4 minutes. Transfer the prepared waffle to a plate in the warm oven. Continue making waffles with the remaining batter.

4— Make the chicken: In a large mixing bowl, combine the flour and seasoning until well mixed.

5— In a separate bowl, pour in the Buffalo sauce.

6— Heat about 3 inches of oil in a heavy pot or Dutch oven over medium-high heat until the temperature reaches 350°F. Line a plate with paper towels.

7— Working in batches, dip the thawed vegan chicken into the Buffalo sauce and then into the flour mixture. Slip into the oil to fry for 4 minutes, or until crispy.

8— Drain on the paper towel–lined plate. Repeat with the remaining chicken.

9— Prep the plates by placing a waffle in the center of each plate and topping with two pieces of fried chicken. Serve immediately with plenty of warmed maple syrup.

BREAKFAST SANDWICH BUSSDOWNS

aka Sausage, Bacon, and Cheesy Egg Pancake Stack Thangs

In this sandwich, the pancakes are your bread. So you're gonna need to make two flapjacks per sandwich. Hungry Jack is my favorite mix personally, but go ahead and use whatever vegan pancake mix is your go-to. Or if you're more ambitious, you can use the waffle batter from Chicken 'n' Waffle Bussdowns (page 92) as a homemade pancake batter. This recipe technically serves four, but good luck not eating all of them yourself.

1— In a large skillet, heat 2 tablespoons of the olive oil over medium heat until shimmering. Add the vegan bacon and cook for 2 to 3 minutes per side, until crispy. Set aside.

2— Add the remaining 2 tablespoons of olive oil to the pan and heat until shimmering. Add the vegan sausage patties and cook for 2 minutes on each side. Set aside.

3— Wipe out the skillet, add the vegan butter and melt over medium heat. Add the vegan eggs, season with salt and pepper, and scramble until firm, about 2 minutes. Lay the sliced vegan cheese over the eggs and cover the pan so it melts.

4— To assemble the bussdowns, place one flapjack on each of four plates. Top each flapjack with a quarter of the eggs and cheese. Top each with a vegan sausage patty and two slices of vegan bacon. Drizzle each with 1 tablespoon of maple syrup. Top with another flapjack. Serve immediately.

SERVES 4

8 flapjacks or pancakes from your favorite mix, prepared according to the package instructions

4 tablespoons olive oil

8 slices vegan bacon, preferably Umaro

4 vegan breakfast sausage patties, preferably Beyond Meat or Impossible

3 tablespoons vegan butter, preferably Earth Balance

2 cups vegan egg substitute, preferably Just Egg

Kosher salt and freshly ground black pepper

4 slices vegan American cheese, preferably Follow Your Heart

4 tablespoons pure maple syrup

BUFFALO CHICKEN-FRIED MUSHROOM PO' BOYS

This is one of my favorite sandwiches to make because the flavor is just like the Buffalo chicken sandwiches I loved eating when I wasn't vegan. For the bread, try to find a French roll that's about six inches long and has a good crumb that can soak up the juices. You can make the slaw and the Cajun sauce about a day or two ahead of time. I recommend making some of our bussin'-ass Mob Ranch (page 146) and dipping your sandwich right in. Serve with some fries on the side. You're gonna be licking ya lips all night.

1— Preheat the oven to 350°F.

2— Split each French roll and toast in the oven until bread is warmed through and crusty on the outside, about 7 minutes. Remove from oven to let cool.

3— When rolls are cool enough to handle, spread half of the vegan mayonnaise on the inside of each roll.

4— Add half of the mushrooms to each roll and top each with half of the slaw and half of the Cajun sauce.

5— Sprinkle each with the green onions and close the rolls.

6— Serve immediately.

SERVES 2

2 French rolls

3 tablespoons vegan mayonnaise

Buffalo Chicken-Fried Mushrooms (page 204), warmed

¾ cup Tasha's Slaw (page 57)

¼ cup Creamy Cajun Mob Sauce (page 145)

¼ cup sliced green onions, white and green parts

CLASSIC FRIED SHRIMP PO' BOY

This is one of the originals of the Vegan Mob menu and it has a very special meaning for me. On the menu we call it the Renz, named after a good friend I was going to start a food truck with before I had a restaurant. We never got to open that truck because he passed away after an overdose. I put this po' boy on the menu in honor of him.

1 — Preheat the oven to 350°F.

2 — Split open each French roll and toast it in the oven until the bread is warmed through and crusty on the outside, about 7 minutes. Remove from oven.

3 — When the rolls are cool enough to handle, spread 1¼ tablespoons of the vegan mayonnaise on the inside of each roll.

4 — Add the shrimp to the rolls and top with slaw and Creamy Cajun Sauce split evenly among all of the sandwiches.

5 — Sprinkle each with the green onions and close the rolls.

6 — Serve immediately.

MAKES 4 PO' BOYS

1 recipe classic fried shrimp (page 75)

4 French rolls

5 tablespoons vegan mayonnaise

1 cup Tasha's Slaw (page 57)

½ cup Creamy Cajun Mob Sauce (page 145)

½ cup sliced green onions

KIDS' TURKEY MOB MELT

This sandwich is inspired by my youngest daughter. She doesn't eat meat anymore, and sometimes it's hard to find a way to make sandwiches for her school lunch. I came up with this sandwich so she wouldn't feel left out at the lunch table. This is something you can do for your kids' lunchboxes, too, or for yourself when you're looking for a quick lunch.

1 — In a large skillet, melt ½ tablespoon of the vegan butter over medium-high heat. Add the vegan bacon and cook for 3 to 4 minutes, until crisp. Set aside.

2 — In the same skillet, brown 1 tablespoon of the vegan butter over medium heat, about 2 minutes.

3 — Add two slices of sourdough bread. Top each of the slices with two slices of vegan turkey, two pieces of bacon, and two slices of vegan cheese. Top each with other slice of bread.

4 — Using a spatula, flip the sandwiches over in pan and cook until the bread is golden brown on both sides and the cheese is melted, about 4 minutes.

5 — Serve immediately or wrap in parchment or aluminum foil and refrigerate until ready to pack lunchboxes.

SERVES 2

2½ tablespoons vegan butter, preferably Earth Balance

4 slices vegan bacon, preferably Umaro

4 slices sourdough bread

8 slices vegan deli turkey, preferably Tofurkey

2 slices vegan American cheese, preferably Follow Your Heart

GOOD OL' AMERICAN DOGS

A Good Ol' American Dog reminds me of the good ol' days when I'd watch my grandmother make a hot dog for herself and put chopped onions, chopped tomatoes, relish, ketchup, and mustard on top before opening up a bag of Lay's potato chips as a snack on the side. You can eat it how you like it, but I recommend cooking on the grill for a smoky taste.

1 — Heat your grill, if using, until the charcoal is grey. Place the vegan hot dogs on grill.

2 — Grill for 1 to 2 minutes on each side, or the until dogs start to blister and the skins burst. Remove from the heat and transfer to a plate.

3 — Split open the hot dog buns and lay them down on the grill to lightly toast them. Remove from the grill and add one half slice of vegan cheese to each bun to melt.

4 — Add the hot dogs to buns and serve alongside condiments.

SERVES 4

4 vegan hot dogs, preferably Lightlife

4 vegan hot dog buns

2 slices vegan cheddar-style cheese, preferably Daiya, halved lengthwise

½ large red onion, diced

TO SERVE

1 medium red tomato, finely diced

Plenty of Best Fry Sauce (recipe on page 142)

Ketchup

Mustard

Vegan mayonnaise

DEEP-FRIED GRILLED CHEESEBURGERS

SERVES 2

I'm not even gonna lie to you . . . this recipe came out of the munchies. I was thinking, "What if a deep-fried grilled cheese had a burger in it?" When I added it to the menu, people loved it. I serve it with French fries and Creamy Cajun Mob Sauce for dipping.

BURGER PATTIES

2 vegan meat patties, preferably Impossible Burger patties

Garlic powder

Onion powder

Kosher salt and freshly ground black pepper

2 teaspoons olive oil for frying

SANDWICHES

4 slices Texas Toast–style thick-sliced bread or your favorite vegan bread

4 slices vegan cheese, preferably any Follow Your Heart cheese

¼ cup chopped green onions, white and green parts

BATTER

½ cup all-purpose flour

1 tablespoon Creole seasoning, preferably Tony Chachere's Original

2 cups water

1 cup panko breadcrumbs

Vegetable oil for frying

TO SERVE

1 cup shredded lettuce

4 tomato slices

2 (¼-inch) red onion slices

¼ cup chopped green onions, white and green parts

Creamy Cajun Mob Sauce (page 145)

1 — Prepare the burger patties: Season the patties on both sides with a sprinkling of garlic powder, onion powder, salt, and pepper. Set aside.

2 — Top two slices of Texas Toast each with a slice of vegan cheese and one-quarter of the green onions; then close them up with the remaining two slices of bread to make sandwiches.

3 — Make the batter: In a large bowl that can fit the whole sandwich, whisk together the flour and Creole seasoning. While whisking, pour in the water and whisk continuously until you have a smooth batter with a consistency similar to cake batter. Dip the sandwiches in the batter, coating them fully. Then fully coat each battered sandwich in panko breadcrumbs and set aside.

4 — Fill a medium heavy skillet with about 3 inches of vegetable oil (it should be high enough that the sandwiches can be almost fully submerged). Heat on medium-high until it reaches 350°F. Line a plate with paper towels.

5 — Meanwhile, in another medium skillet, heat the olive oil over medium heat until shimmering. Add the burger patties and cook for about 5 minutes, turning once. Set aside.

6 — Transfer the battered and breaded sandwiches to the vegetable oil. Fry on both sides until golden brown, about 3 minutes per side. Remove from the oil and drain on the paper towel–lined plate.

7 — Open the deep-fried sandwiches and add a burger patty to each. Garnish with lettuce, tomato, onion, remaining green onion and Creamy Cajun Mob Sauce and serve immediately.

SMACKIN' MACKIN' POTATO TACOS

For y'all who don't wanna do the fake meat, we got y'all covered with this recipe. This right here gonna have you right—it's gonna fill you up and you're gonna love it. These tacos go hella good with the works: salsa (page 199), Guap-amole (page 183), your favorite vegan sour cream, tomatoes, and green onions. You can even pull these out when you have guests over and make a dope-ass taco bar. Throw some hot sauce on it if you wanna turn up the heat a notch.

1— Heat the olive oil in a medium sauté pan over medium heat until shimmering.

2— Add the potatoes, bell pepper, onion and Creole seasoning and sauté for about 10 minutes, until all vegetables are tender, stirring frequently.

3— In a separate medium sauté pan, warm the tortillas one at a time until pliable. Top each with some of the vegan cheddar cheese and allow the cheese to melt.

4— When ready to serve, divide the mixed vegetables evenly among the tortillas. Garnish each with 1 tablespoon of sour cream, 1 tablespoon of tomatoes, and a sprinkling of cilantro and green onions. Serve immediately.

SERVES 2 AS AN ENTRÉE, 3 AS AN APPETIZER

2 tablespoons olive oil

1 pound red creamer potatoes, finely diced

1 red bell pepper, seeded and diced

½ large white onion, diced

1 tablespoon Creole seasoning, preferably Tony Chachere's Original

6 (5-inch) vegan flour tortillas

1 (7-ounce) package shredded vegan cheddar-style cheese, such as Daiya

TO SERVE

6 tablespoons vegan sour cream, preferably Tofutti

6 tablespoons chopped tomatoes

3 tablespoons chopped fresh cilantro leaves

3 green onions, white and green parts, chopped

BREAKFAST MOB WRAP

I came up with this when I was hungry one morning and didn't have much time to sit down and eat. I used to go and get breakfast wraps when I wasn't vegan, and I wanted to do something plant-based. This is something you can make for yourself or for your kids when you need a breakfast that you can take on the go.

SERVES 2

4 tablespoons olive oil,
plus more as needed

2 vegan sweet or hot Italian sausage links, preferably Beyond Meat

2 vegan breakfast sausage patties, preferably Impossible

4 strips vegan bacon, preferably Umaro

4 slices vegan American cheese, preferably Follow Your Heart

6 tablespoons vegan butter, preferably Earth Balance

1 cup vegan egg substitute, preferably Just Egg

Kosher salt and freshly ground black pepper

2 (12-inch) vegan flour tortillas

2 frozen hash brown patties, prepared according to package instructions

TO SERVE

Guap-amole (page 183)

Salsa

Ketchup

Vegan sour cream, preferably Tofutti

1— Make the sausages and bacon: Heat the olive oil in a medium skillet over medium heat until shimmering. Add the vegan Italian sausage links and cook for 3 minutes on each side, until browned. Remove and set aside on a plate. Cook the vegan breakfast sausage patties in the same pan until cooked through, about 5 minutes. Transfer to the plate with the sausage links. Cook the vegan bacon in the same pan, adding more olive oil if needed, for 3 to 4 minutes, until crisp.

2— Place the bacon on top of the sausages and top with the sliced vegan American cheese. Cover and let sit until the cheese melts, about 4 minutes.

3— Make the eggs: In a medium sauté pan, melt the vegan butter over medium heat. Add the vegan egg mixture and scramble using a rubber spatula until solid curdles form, about 5 minutes. Add salt and pepper to taste. Set aside.

4— Assemble the wraps: Lay the tortillas on a work surface. Divide the sausages and bacon with melted cheese, hash browns, and scrambled eggs between the tortillas, keeping the filling towards the center of the wrap.

5— Bring the left and right sides of the tortilla towards one another. Grip the bottom of the wrap and begin rolling upwards, making sure to keep filling inside.

6— Heat a sauté pan over medium heat with a little olive oil until shimmering. Add the wraps to the pan and move frequently until crisp on all sides, 1 to 2 minutes per side.

7— Serve wraps immediately with salsa, vegan sour cream, guacamole, and ketchup on the side for dipping.

"WHAT I'VE LEARNED OVER THE COURSE OF RUNNING VEGAN MOB:

MY FAITH IS UNSHAKABLE, AND I WILL ALWAYS GO FOR MY DREAMS."

THE BEGINNINGS OF VEGAN MOB

and Mob Dishes and Sauces

I try to keep my frequency high and stay focused on positive things so I can bring the right energy to what I do. I'm putting the joy and the love that I get out of cooking and eating Vegan Mob out into the universe, and people are gravitating toward my energy. It radiates out from there to more people all the time, the rap community, my home community—everybody.

Looking back, Vegan Mob's success as a brick-and-mortar is funny because I never planned to have a restaurant, but I *believed* I could have one. Back in 2018 I was in grad school at California Institute of Integral Studies to get a job as a therapist. It was the beginning of my program, and I needed hours in the therapy field to graduate and was looking for something that would allow me to get paid while I did so. I remember the phone call where I got the job offer: it was a middle school in Oakland where my mother-in-law worked. I'd been reaching out to them for about a month, and they'd made room for me to join the team. The pay was going to be $80,000 a year with a guaranteed spot after graduating. I'd be working as a guidance counselor with children who grew up just like me in the Bay Area. Getting that experience and doing it for a couple of years would allow me to be able to open my own therapy practice one day. It was step one on a long staircase, and I saw my future self at the end of it. At the time I thought it was my dream job and it seemed perfect.

But there was something in my heart and in my stomach that told me it wasn't the right move. I didn't want to follow the money that I know would have my family financially secure—I wanted to follow a calling and my happiness. I wanted a more fruitful life. My grad school counselors and professors thought I was crazy to want to leave grad school and turn down that job. But I knew if I was willing to walk away, I'd have to go for the unbelievable dream, and the thing that felt unattainable. So, I followed my gut.

I dropped out of grad school. My mom definitely didn't see the vision at first. She was upset because she was big on education, and I was on track to be her first child that graduated from grad school. For my grandmother, who went to grad school, education was a big part of her family since it wasn't afforded to her parents when they were growing up. School was very important to my grandmother and her sisters, and they thought if you didn't go to school you were doomed.

When my mom asked me why I left and turned down that job, I used her own words on her: "You told me to have faith." It's interesting to think about that moment and that conversation now because she actually ended up super happy when Vegan Mob opened.

While I was in grad school, I worked as an Uber driver. From October 2018 to March 2019, I drove people all around the Bay, from San Francisco to Oakland and all over. I was still working on my dream of owning my own business, so I listened to books about manifestation while I was driving, like *The Secret* by Rhonda Byrne, *Ask and It Is Given* by Esther Hicks and Jerry Hicks, and *Think and Grow Rich* by Napoleon Hill. I learned about the law of attraction and how the energy you bring to your dreams can affect the outcome. The authors talked about how intention and your thinking can impact your life for the better. That's when things changed for me. I started to think about what I wanted to do in life, and I realized I wanted to cook food and do music. I thought about where I wanted to be constantly—it was my singular focus.

Back then, my big plan was to eventually open a food truck. But one day while I was driving for Uber, I thought to myself, "I wish I had a restaurant." I also started to think about how I could use being an Uber driver as a platform to reach my next goals. When I talked to my riders, I learned that a lot of them worked in tech or for startups. They were also working on a dream or trying to reach their goals for their own or someone else's company, and I thought it could be beneficial to talk to them about mine. I started to see each ride as an opportunity for free promotion. I told passengers about Vegan Mob, and I even offered to do catering for their company events and give them a 10 percent discount off their first order. It worked, and I gained hundreds of followers on my social media accounts that way.

Back when I was driving Uber, I was living in Oakland in the Fruitvale district. Fruitvale is a thirty-minute drive from San Francisco, but it reminded me of the hood I grew up in. The Dimond District in particular felt like Divisadero Street back in the day: lots of businesses and residential buildings, but also walkable, and everybody kind of knew everybody. It was like a family vibe. Going to the grocery store, I'd always run into someone I knew. I felt at home in Fruitvale, and people were cool in the neighborhood. That's how I met Chef GW Chew.

Chef GW Chew is an innovator and business owner who lives in Oakland. He grew up in Maryland but moved to the Bay, and he's been vegan for fifteen years. He had a vegan restaurant in the Upper Dimond called The Veg Hub that I ate at all the time. It was really good vegan food, so I asked him where he was getting his proteins. Turned out Chef Chew was making his own from scratch. I was impressed because they were so good. He hooked me up right then and there. I started buying proteins from him and playing around with making my own vegan barbecue at my house. He does such a good job with flavor and texture with each vegan protein. His proteins are my favorite to use to this day.

Not long after that, I was standing at my smoker in my backyard with Chef Chew's own Better Chew steak on the grates, trying to recreate my family's brisket. I smoked it for a long time over hickory wood—for like ten hours—to be sure that it had plenty of smoky flavor. When I tasted it, it was smoky . . . too smoky, and worse, it was dry. It wasn't that bad; it just wasn't as good as I knew it could be. I adjusted the timing so it would cook a little faster and be on the heat for just four hours. I kept testing, trying Beyond vegan sausage links, experimenting with smoking them just like I would real meat links. I've cooked with Beyond links before and was really familiar with the cooking time, so my first version of that came out pretty good, I have to say.

Those backyard days were cool. I had a barbecue grill, a big-ass one with a blue dome. I would be out there testing and looking for the same textures and smells as when I cooked meat barbecue. My neighbors actually complained about the smoke coming into their house next door, so I had to figure out how to change up the method. I had to combine two vegan proteins to cut down on time: I put the links on top of the brisket and let them smoke for four hours. It felt authentic, like how we used to cook at home when I was growing up. I feel like that kind of situation is how you get the best taste out of something.

I was figuring it out, but I needed a name for my new venture. I had started a hashtag called #mobkitchen. I would say "mob" about everything all the time . . . that's just Bay culture. Believe me when I tell you I been saying "mob" since I was a teenager. I tried out the name "Veggie Mob," but my friend said it didn't sound hard enough. He was right, so I changed the name to "Vegan Mob," and what do you know—it stuck.

Once I got more comfortable, I started using social media to share pictures of what I was cooking, and selling plates from the trunk of my Prius. Back in those days, I would drive all around the Bay Area dropping off plates and barbequitos. Moya, an Ethiopian restaurant in downtown San Francisco, reached out to me on Instagram to say they liked what I was doing. They invited me to take over their restaurant for a day and give them a cut, kind of like renting out the space for the evening. I had no idea what I was doing, but I made $3,000 in about six hours, so I knew I had something I could keep going. It was crazy to see it coming together.

One day Chef Chew called me and said he wasn't going to be able to do his farmers market slot anymore, so he offered it to me. He had been selling his vegan plates and thought it would be good for another vegan business to cover for him, and he wanted to help me get my business off the ground. I took him up on it, and he showed me how to set up; trained me for like four hours. He even let me borrow his grill.

The Friday before that first farmers market was crazy. I was up all night in my kitchen making dishes to take with me. I decided I would only sell Mob plates of smoked brisket, green beans, collard greens, Smackaroni and Cheese, and side orders of gumbo with white rice. I was hella anxious that first Sunday morning. I packed up my little Prius and put the trays of food in there with some tables, a sign, chafing dishes, and to-go containers. If you know anything about San Francisco streets and how hilly and curvy they are, you *know* my backseat got so messy by the time I got to the market.

To make matters worse, I got there at 9:30 a.m. The market started at 10, so I didn't have enough time to set up properly. It started out slow, thank goodness, but eventually people rolled in. The line got long quick because I was by myself and trying to do everything on my own: take orders, cook, and package everything. In true SF fashion, the weather took a turn and got windy. Next thing you know, the propane tank that was heating the stove and flattop went out. A fucking tent blew like 30 feet. It was nuts. I was eventually able to get my burner working again, but it took time. I felt like I was barely keeping it together.

I was also nervous because this was a totally different group of consumers than I was used to, and I didn't know how they were going to react. I wanted them to love it so bad. The reactions were actually really positive—a lot of people told me that they didn't believe it was vegan. I thought the first few people who said that were just gassing me up, but after enough people agreed, I started to feel like this was real. After that day, I had a definite answer: I could make Vegan Mob work if I just started hustling to sell as many plates as possible.

I did a few more days at the farmers markets and got better at running it. After a few weeks, people really started to line up. My wife would sometimes be a cashier, but it was still tough and hard to do all the physical labor by myself. I love cooking, but I don't miss working with such a small team with orders piling up, just me and my wife trying to work together to get it all done. But the passion and the love were in the food then, just like now.

I expanded the menu to things like Da Divisadero aka Not-Yo-Cheesesteak, the Mob Link sandwich, and Mob Nachos. I also kept the classics, like the Mob Plate with one vegan meat and three sides and occasionally gumbo. Looking back, actually, it was too much. The wait time for folks was like 15 minutes, because it was just me cooking. But I knew I could do it.

From there, I started setting up at certain locations on weekends, and I would tell people via social media. I started thinking to myself, "Well, instead of a food truck, maybe I should have a restaurant. People want this food." It's funny how life works, because I swear to you, soon after, that thought became a reality. My boy Evan Kidera, who has owned his own food trucks and restaurants in the Bay for twelve years (he currently runs Señor Sisig), hit me up one morning and told me about a restaurant space he was going to be in. He said that when he looked at the spot, he'd thought of me. He really liked the spot, but he felt like it belonged to Vegan Mob.

Fast-forward a few months to Vegan Mob's grand opening. We had a line of over a thousand people, and we made over $20,000 in sales. That first week was fucking crazy. I'm just being real. It was crazy as shit. I'm not even sure I remember everything from our first day, because I was just trying to get through it. We didn't know what to expect. I mean, I knew it would be nuts because of my social media attention, but it was beyond anything I expected. Our second day was a Tuesday, and I remember thinking, "Tuesday is going to be much, much easier."

It wasn't. My cousin had recently passed away, and the second day of us being open—Tuesday—was his funeral. I wasn't going to miss it. I tried to set up my kitchen manager as best as I could so I could leave. I went to the funeral and was heading back to the restaurant when my wife called. She was at the restaurant, and she sounded panicked. She was like, "Yo, you need to get over here now."

By the time I got to the shop, she was in the kitchen, packing orders up, trying to help the staff serve the line of customers that were in front, and making the new orders that kept coming in. She had just stopped by to check on things; she thought she might get some food herself, but things were so crazy that she ended up working. She wanted to help, don't get me wrong, but she was looking so stressed out. As soon as I got there, I jumped in and didn't stop until we finished that day's service. Shit was bananas.

The first week pretty much continued like that. It was great, but I didn't expect it to be that insane. It was pretty rough, because it never really stopped. Each day came with big long lines—it felt like the grand opening over and over again. It's still busy now, but it doesn't feel as crazy. Nowadays we have an order to how we do things and a system in place to handle the number of sales. They say that as a restaurant owner, it'll take two years before your restaurant is running smoothly and you turn a profit, but we've been lucky. It's been good for us from the beginning because it's never slowed down.

Looking back, I wish I'd had more time to plan for a restaurant. If I could do it again, I would definitely take more time to organize and prepare before opening instead of trying to figure it out as I went. When I was selling my Mob meals, I started with just myself, my wife, and these recipes. It's totally different now because I've got a management team, an operations team, and all these layers of support to help us run smoothly. I didn't have any of that in the beginning, and it's been a learning curve for sure. We're also still learning in real time, and I know I'm lucky to have that. Experience is better than guessing, you know?

What sets us apart at Vegan Mob is our uniqueness, quality, and flavor. The dishes are all ones I've come up with in-house, and I've tasted them myself to make sure the flavors are on point. Even when I'm planning posts and content for social media projects, I'm thinking of the values that got me started and how I can convey them to our followers. And even though we're successful, we're still improving and trying to get better—and that includes making the food better. I don't ever want to stop doing that.

I'm a firm believer that what you put out into the world is what you get back. I got that from *The Law of Attraction* and from learning about mindfulness. I try to keep my frequency high and stay focused on positive things so I can bring the right energy to what I do. I'm putting the joy and the love that I get out of cooking and eating Vegan Mob out into the universe, and people are gravitating toward my energy. It radiates out from there to more people all the time, the rap community, my home community—everybody.

My mom was so suspicious of all this at the beginning, but now she's happy. She's happy because she sees me doing my thing and living my dream. The articles, the buzz, the customers, all of it was such a surprise to her and my family who were so worried when I dropped out of grad school. But now they believe.

MOB BURGERS

This is one of the best sellers at Vegan Mob. This burger may be vegan, but it hits all of the notes you'd expect from a beef burger: it's got a salty bite, melty cheese, tartness from the slaw, and creaminess from the vegan mayonnaise. Make a big batch and serve these at a party, and they'll definitely be a hit. Double up the patties and add three slices of vegan bacon to make it a Bela Burger like we serve at the restaurant.

1— In a sauté pan or cast-iron skillet, heat the olive oil over medium heat until shimmering. Add the onion and sauté for about 8 minutes, or until golden. Remove the onions from the pan and set aside.

2— Season each vegan burger patty with the seasoned salt on both sides. Add to the sauté pan or to a heated grill (if grilling). Cook for 3 minutes on one side, until browned. Carefully flip the patties, being sure to lift any crust that has formed on the pan. Top each flipped burger with one vegan cheese slice. Let cook for 2½ minutes, until the cheese melts. Remove the burgers from the pan and set on a plate.

3— In the same pan or on the grill over medium-high heat, toast the hamburger buns until golden brown, about 2 minutes.

4— Spread the bottom of each bun with vegan mayonnaise and the top with Mob Sauce. Add a patty to the bottom half of each bun and top with the onions, tomato slices, and Tasha's Slaw. Serve immediately.

SERVES 4

2 tablespoons olive oil

½ yellow onion, thinly sliced

4 vegan burger patties, preferably Impossible

3 tablespoons seasoned salt, preferably Lawry's

4 vegan American cheese slices, preferably Follow Your Heart

4 vegan hamburger buns, sliced open

5 tablespoons vegan mayonnaise

½ cup Mob Sauce (page 147)

1 tomato, sliced into thin rounds

1 cup Tasha's Slaw (page 57)

MOB BURGER BOWLS

This recipe is for all my folks tryna lose some weight, but still wanting something good to eat. You can still have a burger, just take the bread out, add some veggies, and we mobbin'. You can also have it with some tortilla chips on the side. It's a choose-your-own-adventure meal where you can have it for lunch, for dinner, or as a snack.

1— Divide the lettuce between two bowls. Set aside.

2— Heat the olive oil in a nonstick pan over medium heat until shimmering.

3— Season the vegan burger patties with seasoning salt on both sides and add to the pan. Fry for about 3 minutes until browned, and flip. Place a vegan cheese slice on each patty and continue to cook for 3 minutes, until the cheese melts. Remove the patties from the pan and set aside.

4— Add the onions to pan with the salt and pepper and sauté for 8 minutes, or until golden.

5— In each bowl, add a burger patty on top of the lettuce. Top with the sautéed onions and tomatoes. Drizzle with Mob Sauce and Mob Ranch. Serve immediately.

SERVES 2

2 cups shredded iceberg lettuce

2 vegan burger patties, preferably Impossible Meat

1 tablespoon olive oil

Seasoning salt, preferably Lawry's

2 vegan American cheese slices, preferably Follow Your Heart

½ cup finely diced yellow onion

1 teaspoon kosher salt

1 teaspoon freshly ground black pepper

1 whole tomato, finely diced

Mob Sauce (page 147) for serving

Mob Ranch (page 146) for serving

NACHO CHEESE SAUCE

When I created this nacho cheese sauce, I just started going crazy with it, putting it on nachos, a vegan cheesesteak, a sandwich, fries, and adding it to tacos. This nacho cheese can be used anywhere your creativity takes you, even a baked potato. If you want to make a five-layer dip, add this nacho cheese sauce to it. Or just grab your favorite tortilla chips and dip them into this. It's a great snack.

Note: You may notice that I call for slices and shreds here. That's for good reason: Shreds melt different than the slices. The slices melt smoothly, and the shreds have more of a custardy type of melt. The combination brings out an extra-cheesy look and taste.

1— Melt the vegan butter in a large pot over medium heat. Add the green onions and garlic and sauté until softened, about 2 minutes. Add the flour and cook, stirring with a whisk occasionally, until flour is slightly toasted and has a nutty aroma, about 3 minutes.

2— While whisking, pour in the pea milk and continue to cook until sauce is thickened and smooth, about 5 minutes. Make sure to run whisk along the edges of the pot to get all of the flour.

3— Turn the heat down to low and add the salt, the chopped vegan cheese, and the cheddar shreds. Cook for about 5 minutes, stirring occasionally, until most of the shredded cheese is melted. If the sauce is still lumpy, add hot water, ¼ cup at a time, and whisk until smooth.

4— Drain the jalapeño slices, reserving the liquid. Add 1 cup of the liquid and whisk to incorporate.

5— Serve warm with plenty of tortilla chips and top with some jalapeño slices.

MAKES 4 CUPS (SERVES 8)

1 stick (8 tablespoons) vegan butter, preferably Earth Balance

1 cup chopped green onions, white and green parts

2 tablespoons minced garlic

½ cup all-purpose flour

2½ cups unsweetened pea milk, preferably Ripple

1 tablespoon kosher salt, plus more to taste

2 (7.8-ounce) packages vegan cheddar-style cheese slices, preferably Daiya, coarsely chopped

1 (8-ounce) bag vegan cheddar shreds

Hot water, as needed

1 (18-ounce) jar hot jalapeño slices

Tortilla chips for serving

UNCLE MOBBY'S (BOBBY'S) GREEN BEANS

My Uncle Bobby taught me how to make these green beans, straight from Houston, Texas, and it changed my life. The flavors were incredible. Now I make this vegan version, and my mom asks me to make them every year at the holidays. Serve these with your favorite Mob main.

1— Heat the olive oil in a large sauté pan over medium heat until shimmering. Add the garlic, onion, and green and red bell peppers and sauté until tender, 5 to 7 minutes.

2— Add the chopped vegan bacon to the pan and sauté for a few minutes, until the veggies are soft. Add the veggie broth and green beans, increase the heat to high, and cook until the mixture comes to a boil.

3— Add the salt and pepper and decrease the heat to medium low. Cover and let simmer for 30 minutes or until the beans are tender and falling apart.

4— Serve immediately.

SERVES 4

1 tablespoon olive oil

1 tablespoon chopped garlic

1 yellow onion, chopped

1 green bell pepper, diced

1 red bell pepper, diced

4 slices smoked vegan bacon, preferably Umaro, chopped

2 cups vegetable broth

1 pound fresh green beans, trimmed

2 tablespoons pink Himalayan salt

1 tablespoon freshly ground black pepper

MY MOMMA'S BRUSSELS SPROUTS

My mom always liked to keep things interesting in the kitchen, making different types of food and trying different recipes. I never really liked brussels sprouts that much until my mom made these. They're really good and make a good side for fried chicken. Add some Smackaroni and Cheese (page 38) and Mobby Garlic Bread (page 48) for a good dinner.

1 — Preheat the oven to 450°F.

2 — On a baking sheet, toss the brussels sprouts and pecans with the olive oil, salt, and pepper. Spread out in a single layer.

3 — Bake for 20 to 25 minutes, until the sprouts are browned and tender. Serve immediately.

SERVES 4

1 pound brussels sprouts, trimmed and halved

½ cup pecans, chopped

2 tablespoons olive oil

1 teaspoon kosher salt

1 teaspoon freshly ground black pepper

1 medium garlic clove, thinly sliced

MOB "CLAM" CHOWDER

Growing up in Frisco, I've always loved clam chowder. I think we probably have the best in the world. Before I was vegan, I used to go to Pier 39 in the downtown area of Frisco and get chowder in a bread bowl and eat it in a little outside booth. This version is vegan but still hits those same notes.

1— In a large heavy pot or Dutch oven, heat the olive oil over medium heat until shimmering.

2— Add the potatoes and sauté until softened and lightly browned, about 5 minutes.

3— Add the vegan butter, garlic, mushrooms, celery, and onion to the pot and stir. Decrease the heat to medium low. Sauté for 3 minutes, until the onion is translucent.

4— Add the flour and stir to coat the vegetables. Let cook until flour becomes light brown and smells toasted, about 2 minutes.

5— Add the vegan heavy cream, making sure to scrape up any flour that has stuck to the bottom of the pot. Add the vegetable broth and continue to stir until the cream and broth are well combined.

6— Cover the pot and let cook for 30 minutes. Every 5 minutes or so, check the pot to make sure it's not boiling and turn the heat down, if necessary. Give the vegetables a stir, too.

7— After 30 minutes, test the vegetables and make sure they're tender. If not, cover and cook for another 10 minutes and check again. Taste and adjust seasoning with salt and pepper. Stir in the parsley. Serve immediately.

MAKES 4 CUPS (SERVES 4)

2 tablespoons olive oil

2 red potatoes, diced

1 stick (8 tablespoons) vegan butter, preferably Earth Balance

2 garlic cloves, minced

1 cup fresh shiitake mushrooms caps, finely chopped

1 celery rib, finely diced

½ white onion, diced

¼ cup all-purpose flour

2 cups vegan unsweetened half-and-half or heavy cream, preferably Ripple

1 cup vegetable broth

Kosher salt and freshly ground black pepper

¼ cup chopped fresh parsley

PICKLED CARROTS

I hit my mom up for a recipe, and she gave me some game. From her game, I came up with this. You can toss this on your salad or on a nice sandwich. It's nothing but flavor.

1— Combine all ingredients in a medium bowl or in a large mason jar, stirring to make sure the sugar is dissolved. Cover and let sit overnight in the refrigerator.

2— Serve cold, and refrigerate leftovers covered for up to a week.

MAKES 2 CUPS

¾ pound carrots, shredded on a large grater or mandolin

1 cup white vinegar

½ cup mirin

½ cup soy sauce

½ cup fresh lemon juice

¼ cup granulated sugar

MOMMA GAIL'S GOURMET GREEN BEANS

These green beans: hella good. These are made strictly with veggies, no (vegan) meat. My mom likes to cook vegetables, and she makes them taste hella good without using meat. She always thought using meat to cook vegetables defeated the purpose. I made these and they were good as hell. Pair this up with some garlic noodles (page 164) and some vegan fried shrimp (page 75).

1— In a sauté pan over high heat, heat the olive oil until shimmering. Add the green beans and toss, then keep cooking, making sure they're not browning, until coated in the oil and sizzling, about 5 minutes.

2— Add the water, garlic, and lemon juice and allow to cook, tossing frequently until the water evaporates. Continue to sauté the green beans until soft and browned slightly, about 7 minutes. Add salt and pepper to taste. Serve immediately.

SERVES 4

1 pound fresh green beans, trimmed

3 tablespoons olive oil

½ cup water

4 garlic cloves, chopped

2 tablespoons fresh lemon juice

Kosher salt and freshly ground pepper

"GRILLED" VEGETABLE RICE BOWL

This rice bowl is one of my favorites because it's healthy and delicious. Anytime I'm trying to diet, I'm eating this all day. If you want to, you can even lower the amount of oil and butter for an even healthier meal. This recipe calls for smoked salt, which you can go pick up at Whole Foods. Okay, let's get healthy!

1— In a large skillet over medium heat, heat the olive oil and vegan butter until sputtering. Add the garlic and ginger and mix quickly. Add the zucchini and yellow squash and sauté, tossing frequently, until softened, about 5 minutes.

2— Add the mushrooms and let cook for another 3 minutes until fragrant, making sure to move the pan frequently so the garlic and ginger don't burn.

3— Add the red onion, season with smoked salt and black pepper, and cook for another 5 minutes, until the red onion is a bright burgundy color and the vegetables are soft but not soggy. Serve immediately on top of rice.

SERVES 2

2 tablespoons olive oil

1 tablespoon vegan butter, preferably Earth Balance

2 garlic cloves, sliced

1 teaspoon minced fresh ginger

1 zucchini, cubed

1 yellow squash, cubed

1 pound white mushrooms, halved

1 red onion, sliced

Smoked salt

Freshly ground black pepper

Cooked white rice for serving

G-MONEY MOB SALAD

aka Momma's Salad

My momma always taught me to eat healthy and that you've got to balance out all the things you eat, so let's put some good in our lives with this salad. Although I grew up eating soul food, my mother always ate healthy. She's very versatile, and I truly believe she is where I get my knowledge of food. My momma taught me a lot about culture through food. With my mother being a San Francisco native, that definitely makes a lot of sense, and I'm blessed to have a mother like mine to put me up on a lot of game. Okay, no more mushy shit. You wanna lose some weight and eat clean? Eat this!

1— Make the dressing: In a small bowl, combine the olive oil, lemon juice, salt, pepper, smoked paprika, mustard, honey, and rice vinegar. Whisk together until blended. Set aside.

2— Make the salad: In large bowl, combine the baby kale, arugula, cabbage, cucumber, tomatoes, avocados, shallots, and pickled carrots. Drizzle with half of dressing and toss to coat. Taste and if desired, add additional dressing. Serve immediately. Store additional dressing in an airtight container for up to 3 days.

MAKES 4 CUPS (SERVES 6)

DRESSING

¼ cup olive oil

¼ cup fresh lemon juice

1 teaspoon kosher salt

1 teaspoon freshly ground black pepper

1 teaspoon smoked paprika

1 tablespoon yellow mustard

1 tablespoon honey

½ teaspoon rice wine vinegar

SALAD

2 cups baby kale

1 cup arugula

1 cup shredded purple cabbage

1 cucumber, seeded and diced

2 cups cherry tomatoes, halved

2 ripe avocados, pitted, peeled, and diced

2 shallots, thinly sliced

2 tablespoons Pickled Carrots (page 127)

MOBBY STEAK OMELET

When I used to eat steak and eggs, I felt like it was something special. It's not your everyday meal. Nowadays I'm veganizing it, but I'm still adding the cheese and things. A steak omelet goes crazy with a side of country potatoes and orange juice. I'm getting hungry right now writing this. Grab you some hot sauce and get lit. I'm telling you, this steak omelet is smackin'.

1— Heat the olive oil in a sauté pan over medium heat until shimmering. Add the red and green bell peppers and salt and sauté for 3 minutes, until the vegetables are tender.

2— Add the vegan steak and cook for another 3 minutes, until somewhat browned. Remove the veggies and steak from the pan and set aside.

3— Return the pan to the stove and lower the heat slightly to medium-low. Add the vegan butter to pan and let melt. Add the vegan egg to the pan, stirring briefly with a rubber spatula until curds start to form, about 3 minutes.

4— Stop stirring and add half of the sautéed steak and bell peppers to one half of the omelet. Top with the vegan cheese slices.

5— Using a rubber spatula, fold the opposite half of the omelet over the steak mixture. Carefully flip and let cook on the other side until the cheese melts, about 2 minutes.

6— Place the omelet on a plate and top with remaining steak and bell peppers. Serve immediately.

SERVES 2

1 tablespoon olive oil

½ cup diced red bell pepper

½ cup diced green bell pepper

1 teaspoon kosher salt

½ cup vegan shredded meat, preferably Better Chew shredded steak

2 tablespoons vegan butter, preferably Earth Balance

1 cup vegan egg substitute, preferably Just Egg

2 slices vegan cheddar cheese, preferably Daiya cheddar-style slices

STUFFED SMACKARONI BELL PEPPERS

This is a good way to get the kids to eat something tasty and nutritious. My daughter loves these because they're cheesy and flavorful. The recipe is pretty simple and fun to make with your kids. But even if you don't have kids, you should make this anyway.

Note: You may notice that I call for slices and shreds here. That's for good reason: Shreds melt different than the slices. The slices melt smoothly, and the shreds have more of a custardy type of melt. The combination brings out an extra-cheesy look and taste.

1— Preheat the oven to 350°F. Lightly grease a 9 by 13-inch baking pan.

2— Cook the macaroni in a large pot of boiling salted water per the package instructions. Drain and set aside.

3— Melt the vegan butter in the same pot over medium heat. Add the green onions and garlic and sauté until softened, about 2 minutes. Add the flour and cook, whisking constantly, until flour is slightly toasted, about 3 minutes.

4— While whisking, pour in 4 cups of pea milk and continue to cook until the sauce is thickened and smooth, about 5 minutes. Make sure to run whisk along the edges of the pot to incorporate all of the flour.

5— Turn the heat down to low and add 1 tablespoon kosher salt and both the chopped vegan cheese and the cheese shreds. Cook for about 5 minutes, stirring occasionally, until most of the cheese is melted. If the sauce is still lumpy, add the additional ½ cup of pea milk and whisk until smooth.

6— Add the cooked macaroni and stir well to coat.

7— Pour the macaroni into the greased baking pan. Cover with foil and bake for 20 minutes, or until the sauce is bubbly. Transfer to a wire rack until cool enough to handle. Leave the oven on.

CONTINUED

SERVES 6

SMACKARONI

2 cups (16 ounces) dry elbow macaroni

1 stick (8 tablespoons) vegan butter, preferably Earth Balance

1 cup chopped green onions, white and green parts

2 tablespoons minced garlic

½ cup all-purpose flour

4 to 4½ cups unsweetened pea milk, preferably Ripple

Kosher salt

2 (7-ounce) packs sliced vegan cheddar, preferably Daiya cheddar-style slices, coarsely chopped

1 (7-ounce) package vegan cheddar shreds

STUFFED PEPPERS

6 red bell peppers

1 tablespoon olive oil

2 (12-ounce) packages vegan ground meat, preferably Impossible ground beef

Kosher salt and freshly ground black pepper

STUFFED SMACKARONI BELL PEPPERS,
CONTINUED

8 — Prep the bell peppers by cutting the tops off and using your hands to remove seeds and the white membrane. Rinse each bell pepper and dry. Set aside.

9 — Cook the ground meat: In a large skillet, heat the olive oil over medium heat until shimmering. Add the vegan ground beef and season with salt and pepper. Cook the meat, breaking up lumps with a wooden spoon. Cook until the meat is tender, about 12 minutes, stirring frequently. Set aside.

10 — Assemble the bell peppers: Fill each pepper with ½ cup of Smackaroni and ½ cup of cooked ground meat.

11 — Place the stuffed peppers upright in a second 9 by 13-inch baking pan. Pour ¼ inch of water into the bottom of the pan.

12 — Bake for 30 minutes, until the bell peppers are tender. Remove from the oven and let cool for 10 minutes before serving.

LEMON-SAGE FETTUCCINE WITH MOBBY FRIED CHICKEN

A lot of my ideas for food come to me when I'm a little high, and this lemon sage situation is a perfect example of that. I had the munchies, and as soon as I thought about a delicious sauce drizzled over some pasta with some crispy fried chicken, I went straight to the drawing board, aka my kitchen. Pair this with some of Momma Gail's Gourmet Green Beans (page 129) for a lit vegan dinner.

1— Make the sauce: In a heavy pot or Dutch oven, heat the pea milk over medium-high heat until just simmering, about 5 minutes. Add the vegan parmesan, garlic, vegan butter, Creole seasoning, sage, parsley, and lemon juice. Stir to make sure everything is well mixed. Let cook for about 7 minutes, until the sauce is smooth and the ingredients are well incorporated.

2— Taste and adjust the seasonings with salt and pepper. Keep warm.

3— Make the Mobby Fried Chicken and Mobby Garlic Bread.

4— Make the pasta: Bring a large pot of salted water to a boil. Cook the fettuccine according to the package instructions. Drain well.

5— Evenly divide the pasta among four plates. Place two pieces of hot Mobby Fried Chicken on top of the fettuccine on each plate and top with a ⅓ cup of the sauce. Serve immediately, with a side of warm Mobby Garlic Bread.

SERVES 4

LEMON-SAGE PARMESAN SAUCE

2 cups unsweetened pea milk, preferably Ripple

1 cup grated or shredded vegan parmesan, preferably Follow Your Heart

¼ cup minced garlic

½ stick (4 tablespoons) vegan butter, preferably Earth Balance

1 teaspoon Creole seasoning, preferably Tony Chachere's Original

1 tablespoon chopped fresh sage leaves

¼ cup chopped fresh parsley

3 tablespoons fresh lemon juice

Kosher salt and freshly ground black pepper

TO SERVE

Mobby Fried Chicken (page 50)

Mobby Garlic Bread (page 48), warmed

8 ounces dry fettuccine (should yield 4 cups cooked)

GET YO' SPINACH AND MUSHROOM QUESADILLA

My mom used to make me quesadillas, and I loved them. One day I went to this popular spot in San Francisco called Pancho Villa Taqueria. They have all type of tacos and burritos, but my favorite is the quesadilla with mushrooms in it. I decided to add spinach when I made my own version to get a little more veggies in. This is good for the kids when you're trying to make them eat their veggies. Pair this up with our salsa (page 199) and go crazy.

1 — Heat the olive oil in a saucepan over medium heat until shimmering. Add mushrooms and salt and sauté for 3 minutes, until slightly softened. Add the garlic and spinach to the pan and sauté until spinach is wilted and garlic is fragrant, about 2 minutes. Set aside.

2 — In a large skillet, melt the vegan butter over medium heat. Add the tortilla to warm and flip so both sides get a coating of vegan butter. With the tortilla still in the pan and add the vegan gouda slices to one half of the tortilla. Top the cheese with the mushroom and spinach mixture. Fold the opposite side of the tortilla over the mixture and carefully flip. Continue cooking until both sides are evenly golden brown and the cheese is melted, about 5 minutes total.

3 — Remove from the pan and cut the quesadilla into four slices. Serve immediately.

SERVES 2 AS AN APPETIZER

1 tablespoon olive oil

¼ cup sliced fresh shiitake mushroom caps

1 teaspoon kosher salt

1 large garlic clove, minced

4 cups spinach

½ tablespoon vegan butter, preferably Earth Balance

1 (12-inch) vegan flour tortilla

2 slices vegan smoked gouda, preferably Follow Your Heart

2 tablespoons vegan mayonnaise

2 tablespoons ketchup

2 tablespoons Sweet Baby Ray's Barbecue Sauce

BEST FRY SAUCE

This smackin' sauce can go with a lot of things: La La Lumpia (page 209), Mobby Fried Chicken (page 50), tacos . . . of course, you read the name, so you know French fries are my favorite things to dip in this. With fries, this sauce can get addicting, so be careful.

In a small bowl, combine the vegan mayo, ketchup, and barbecue sauce. Stir until well blended. Store refrigerated in an airtight container for up to a week.

2 tablespoons chili garlic sauce

1/2 cup soy sauce

1/4 cup white vinegar

BLAZIN' CHILI–GARLIC DIPPING SAUCE

This blazin' sauce will have you singing and dancing. You can slap this sauce on a po' boy (page 98) and let loose, use it as a dip for your vegan fried chicken (page 50), or serve alongside our garlic noodles (page 164). Whichever way you go it's gonna have you hooked.

Mix together the chili garlic sauce, soy sauce, and vinegar in a medium bowl until well combined. Keep refrigerated in an airtight container for up to a week.

MOBBIN'-ASS
BUFFALO SAUCE

CREAMY
CAJUN
MOB SAUCE

MOB RANCH

MOB SAUCE

VEGAN MOB LEMON
PEPPER SAUCE

BLAZIN' CHILI-GARLIC
DIPPING SAUCE

BEST FRY SAUCE

CREAMY CAJUN MOB SAUCE

MAKES 2 CUPS

Sometimes, you have to do stuff on the fly. I came up with this recipe on the day of Vegan Mob's grand opening, with about 30 minutes left until the door opened. I had a po' boy on the menu with no sauce, and I knew it needed something. I just started grabbing ingredients and tossing them together. Today, this sauce is a hit with the whole mob, the guests, and even the family (the staff). Eat this on a po' boy (page 98), with shrimp, fried chicken, sandwiches, or almost anything really.

1½ cups vegan mayonnaise

⅓ cup chili garlic sauce

¼ cup ketchup

2 tablespoons fresh lemon juice

2 tablespoons Mob Sauce (page 145) or any barbecue sauce

Mix together the vegan mayonnaise, chili garlic sauce, ketchup, lemon juice, and Mob Sauce in a medium bowl. Stir until well blended. Keep leftovers refrigerated in an airtight container for up to a week.

VEGAN MOB LEMON PEPPER SAUCE

MAKES 1 CUP

This the sauce for a boss. Use this for Mobby Fried Chicken (page 50), shrimp, pastas, and even veggies. This some gourmet player shit right here.

1 stick (8 tablespoons) vegan butter, preferably Earth Balance

2 tablespoons fresh lemon juice

2 tablespoons lemon pepper

1 — Melt the vegan butter in a small saucepan over medium heat. Add the lemon juice and lemon pepper and stir well to blend.

2 — Let cool and store in an airtight container in the fridge for up to a week.

⅓ cup vegan sour cream,
preferably Tofutti

2 tablespoons vegan mayonnaise

2 tablespoons fresh lemon juice

1 teaspoon Creole seasoning,
preferably Tony Chachere's Original

¼ cup chopped fresh parsley

1 teaspoon kosher salt

1 teaspoon freshly ground black pepper

MOB RANCH

This shit right here is hella good with pizza, Buffalo Chicken-Fried Mushrooms (page 204), Cheeseburger Rolls (page 206), salads, garlic bread, and whatever else you wanna mob it on!

1— Combine the vegan sour cream, vegan mayo, lemon juice, Creole seasoning, and parsley in a medium mixing bowl and stir until well blended. Taste and adjust the seasonings with salt and pepper.

2— Place the bowl in the refrigerator, covered, and keep chilled until ready to serve. Refrigerate leftovers in an airtight container for up to a week.

2 sticks (16 tablespoons) vegan butter,
preferably Earth Balance

2 teaspoons garlic powder

1⅓ cups hot sauce, preferably Crystal
Hot Sauce

MOBBIN'-ASS BUFFALO SAUCE

I don't even need to tell you this recipe is for our Buffalo Chicken-Fried Mushrooms (page 204) . . . or any other kind of vegan Buffalo wings.

1— Melt the vegan butter in a medium pan over medium-low heat. Remove the pan from the heat to prevent scorching.

2— Whisk in the garlic powder and hot sauce until blended, about 1 minute.

3— Serve immediately or let cool and store in the refrigerator in an airtight container for up to two weeks.

MOB SAUCE

Barbecue sauce can make or break barbecue. The meat can be cooked right, but if it's topped with sauce that's not good, it's going to bring the whole thing down. This is my version of classic barbecue sauce. It's tangy, smoky, and it's not hella sweet. At the restaurant, it basically goes on everything, especially the smoked barbecue proteins. It's also hella good with some Mobby Fried Chicken (page 50). I swear you can add it to any burger or sandwich, or dip your French fries in it. It's that good.

This recipe makes a lot, but once you try it, you'll be addicted. I recommend keeping a jar in your fridge, then freezing the rest in smaller servings (like in an ice cube tray) to pull out whenever you need to add flavor to something you're grilling.

5½ cups (48 ounces) tomato sauce

¼ cup ketchup

2 tablespoons yellow mustard

1 cup packed light brown sugar

½ cup minced garlic

½ cup dry sake

½ cup mirin

3 tablespoons soy sauce

¼ cup fresh lemon juice

⅓ cup mesquite liquid smoke

1— Combine the tomato sauce, ketchup, mustard, brown sugar, garlic, sake, mirin, soy sauce, lemon juice, and liquid smoke in a large pot. Bring to a boil over high heat, which should take about 25 minutes.

2— Decrease the heat down to low, partially cover the pot, and let simmer for 2 hours, stirring once every 30 minutes or so, until reduced, thickened, and darker in color.

3— Turn off the heat and let the sauce completely cool on the stovetop. Transfer to airtight containers and store in the fridge overnight before using. This will keep in the fridge for up to a month and in the freezer for up to a year.

"YOU DON'T HAVE TO BE PERFECT, BUT MAKE SURE YOU HAVE A PURE HEART."

"AS TIME GOES ON, THINGS GROW AND CHANGE AND EVOLVE.

I THINK THAT'S A GOOD THING. DON'T LET THE RULES KEEP YOU STAGNANT."

When people hear the word "fusion," they sometimes think of it as a bad thing, but I think it's a good thing. Fusion doesn't mean you have to lose the essence of the original; it just means you are incorporating something else into it and making it even better. You can respect the original sources while also making something new and fun. Fusion embodies a lot of what makes Vegan Mob special. Our wraps, rolls, and bowls mix up different flavors and create a bunch of different textures, but it all works together.

Just as both sides of my family came to the West Coast and made it home, many other groups of immigrants came here and made it their home, too. California has the largest immigrant populations in the country, and that's what makes it feel like a great big melting pot. That's how I see America anyway, just a big melting pot of different cultures. People from different cultures come here and bring their swag, and it mixes with American culture and becomes Americanized. That's true in the food, too, and that's what Vegan Mob is.

The Bay is really a mix of a bunch of different people coming together out on the West Coast, so I try to reflect that on Vegan Mob's menu. My inspiration starts with Black culture and barbecue, but there's also Thai, Chinese, Mexican, and Filipino ingredients on the menu.

When I started cooking it was natural for me to incorporate all of the influences that I grew up with into my food.

Being in the Bay means I have access to many different cultures and can incorporate vegan products from them into my cooking. And a lot of my recipes start with a trip to a store, specifically to different Asian, Mexican, and African shops around the Bay. But Vegan Mob's wraps and rolls came out of a specific tradition that I heard about and was curious about.

When you look at Vegan Mob's menu, you can see it all comes from being a San Francisco native. Here in the Bay, there's not one type of food that everybody eats—we all eat all of it. I want to show love to all of those cultures because I'm a fan of food. Not just the food of my culture, but a fan of food, period.

One day, back when I was driving Uber, I got a passenger who talked to me about how much he loves roti, an Indian flatbread. I had never heard of it before, so I started to do my own research. It looked really good, so I tried to make my own vegan version. I saw pictures of stewed meats and vegetables served on top of the flatbread, open-faced, so I thought I'd try that, but with vegan ingredients and with a barbecue influence because that's what I like to eat. I filled my vegan roti with Smackaroni, shrimp, slaw, and Mob Sauce poured on top. It was good, but it wasn't smackin'. That inspired me to take a burrito wrap and put a lot of stuff inside, like smoked brisket, baked beans, and of course Smackaroni. Now *that* was smackin'. I called it a "barberito" because it was barbecue and it was a burrito. My wife was like, "I think 'barbequito' sounds better." I wanted a second opinion, so I asked Red, my Mexican patna, what sounded better to him. He agreed with my wife—he said, "'Barbequito' sounds Latino with some Black in it," which was funny as hell. So that's what we call it on the menu. It's been on the menu since day one, and it's still one of our top sellers.

To be completely honest, I haven't found any fusion that doesn't work. I go crazy with the wraps. At the restaurant, we have garlic prawn wraps, brisket barbequito wraps, and so many more. It just keeps going, and the combinations keep getting better and better. Our customers respond really well to meals that combine a bunch of different influences. The barbequito, the garlic noodles, the lumpia—my customers love all of that, and they get that I'm trying to be respectful to each culture.

I believe that respectfulness translates to the attention we get—nationwide and even globally—and I think it's also because we are diverse. Maybe it's because we're vegan, maybe it's because we have the soul of soul food but also the different types of dishes that everyone loves. Our diversity shows up in who comes to the restaurant, too. I get my hip-hop followers, my foodies who just want to try something delicious, and my vegans, who have a wide range of different ethnic and racial backgrounds. It's a blend of a bunch of different people, all united behind Vegan Mob.

There's definitely a stereotypical idea of the angry activist vegans or the vegans who think they're healthier than you are or will ever be. That stereotype is also always a white person. I hate that stereotype. Nobody owns being vegan, and there's a lot of people of color around the world who don't eat meat or animal products. Vegan Mob shows that people who look just like me, or like anybody, can be vegan and eat this food. Different types of vegans want to have fun and be cool and hip and diverse. Vegan Mob brings all kinds of people together.

It reminds me of what I love about hip-hop and rap culture. I noticed a long time ago that hip-hop unifies everyone, too, and the vegan food at my restaurant feels like just another form of hip-hop. It's almost like I'm writing a song when I'm cooking, and that's why Vegan Mob's food is fun and hip and expressive. With the music, my creativity comes best when I'm excited about the song and like the beat. The more I really like the beat, the more I get into it, and it comes out naturally. It's the same thing with Vegan Mob. When I'm really excited about a dish, and when I really love something, I'm into it. I try to treat Vegan Mob like an album, and each menu item is a song. I don't want weak songs on my album, so I make sure every song is fire and every song is dope. No skips. I want to create a no-skips menu, too. I want you to be able to go through the whole menu and have all of it be good.

A lot of people think of fusion as something new, but it's actually old. I grew up eating Creole food, which is a fusion of African, French, and native ingredients and cooking techniques coming together into different dishes. It's really the history of the area and a bunch of different cuisines. And now with social media, fusion food is only happening faster, bringing different food to people's attention: one chef sees another chef making something on the other side of the

world and that video or post can inspire them to go into their kitchen and make something new. It's just like in the rap game—everyone is inspired by someone else's style, and then they make it their own.

A perfect example is my top three emcees from the Bay: Too $hort, Mac Dre, and E-40. I was listening to Mac Dre when I was a little kid and got into Too $hort later because, honestly, I just liked his hard-ass music and the way he said his rhymes. My favorite songs by Too $hort are "Dope Fiend Beat" and "Freaky Tales" because those beats go so hard and his flow is crazy. Mac Dre sounded like Too $hort to me, and the first time I heard him, I actually couldn't tell the difference. Once I listened more, I saw he was similar but different from Too $hort, and he built off of that. Mac Dre's music wasn't as violent,

but he was a player; he spoke about game, and he spoke about life. Dre felt like a big brother because his music was teaching me how to carry myself and move through life as a man. The style of music and the content when I started making music sounded like Mac Dre—he was from Vallejo.

Then came E-40. I started listening to him when I was in sixth grade, and I remember hearing how his style was innovative and creative, and he rapped fast. He built a whole empire out of making music, creating his own sound, and later his own wine. Plus, his rhymes have always been good. E-40 now is basically the ambassador of the Bay and reps Vegan Mob hard.

All three are really creative rappers, and they rubbed off on me. Their beats have samples and remixes of songs they grew up listening to. History repeats in cycles, and we make it new by adding a little bit of ourselves to it each time.

Every artist is influenced by other artists, and that's happening in food, too. Black people been doing that in our kitchens forever. Vegan Mob is me, and it speaks to my culture. The fusion of my background and this food that I love shows up on the menu. The garlic noodles and the garlic rice, the tacos, the fried chicken with the sweet chili? That's me showing what I love about the Bay.

There are no rules when it comes to cooking. If you can try it and it works, then you just made something. So many dishes were invented because someone had to get creative with what they had. Chefs are always going to be creating, and if we only stick to the rules and the way things are done, then we'll never get anything new. I remember when my grandmother would watch me make macaroni and cheese and put different meats in it back when I wasn't vegan. She would get pissed off. "That's not how you do it," she would say. You know I love my grandmother, but I disagree. Even OG macaroni and cheese started from someone's imagination.

There wouldn't be vegan barbecue period if someone just said, "That's not how things are done." As time goes on, things grow and change and evolve. I think that's a good thing. Don't let the rules keep you stagnant. If I believed in following the rules, I wouldn't have combined Black food with Mexican food. Sometimes people look at me crazy, like that's not Mexican or that's not Black. I wonder if my grandmother would say, "You don't put no brisket in a burrito." But she would love everything I'm doing and be supportive, even though she would be confused for sure.

As long as you're confined to rules, you're not going to grow. You need to respect other people, but other people's rules about what can be done in music, food, and art are bullshit. Dare to be different. It's natural to be open to trying other things. You may get stuck but that's part of the process, too. You're not going to go to jail. Just try it. It's your kitchen, and you should feel comfortable in there.

I believe that food will continue to evolve, and that flavor and cultural combinations will keep going as long as people continue to want to create and are unafraid. Some things don't last, but ideas that are innovative usually stay around. I think that's always going to happen as long as people are here on this planet. And sometimes when you're trying to make something else and make a mistake, you can actually end up somewhere better. Once when I was trying to make a roti, I messed it up and folded it up instead of leaving it open-faced. I ended up making a dish that I loved. Sometimes you may not have everything you need in your kitchen, so you have to make do. That's fusion, too. Either way, you could end up with something totally different than what you intended to make. Now you gettin' creative.

VEGAN MOB VEGGIE CHOW MEIN

Sometimes you want Chinese food, but you want to make it for yourself. This is my version of veggie chow mein, and it go crazy. When you looking to eat something that'll fill you up and has some nutritional value to it, this is your meal.

1— Cook the noodles according to the package instructions (or, if noodles are pre-cooked, skip this step). Set aside.

2— Heat the olive oil to a large wok over medium heat for 1 minute. Add the vegan butter.

3— Once the butter is melted, add the garlic and stir fry for 2 minutes until the garlic is cooked and fragrant but not browned.

4— Add the red and green bell peppers, broccoli, and onion to the wok and toss with the garlic, making sure the veggies are coated with butter and oil. Cook for 5 minutes, or until the vegetables are tender.

5— Add the cooked noodles and toss to combine with butter and oil. Cook for 3 minutes, until all ingredients are heated through.

6— Add the soy sauce and toss to coat noodles. Let cook for 2 minutes, until hot. Top with the green onions. Serve immediately.

MAKES 4 CUPS (SERVES 4)

2 tablespoons olive oil

1 tablespoon vegan butter, preferably Earth Balance

3 garlic cloves

¾ cup diced red bell pepper

¾ cup diced green bell pepper

1 cup broccoli florets

½ large white onion, sliced

2 cups (1 16-ounce package) packed yakisoba noodles, or 3 cups other cooked vegan Asian noodles

½ cup soy sauce

¼ cup sliced green onions

GOOD-ASS HONEY–WALNUT SHRIMP

Back before I was vegan, I loved ordering honey-walnut shrimp at Chinese restaurants. It's also my wife's favorite, so I make this vegan creamy, crunchy, slightly sweet version. Add some steamed broccoli and Garlic Fried Rice (page 168) and it's a wrap.

1— Prepare the fried shrimp. Set aside.

2— Combine the honey and walnuts in a bowl and mix until the walnuts are evenly coated.

3— Pour this mixture into a nonstick pan over medium heat. Cook, and using a rubber spatula, stir the walnuts until fragrant and slightly browned, about 6 minutes. Remove from the heat and set aside.

4— In a large bowl, combine the vegan mayonnaise and agave. Add the reserved walnut mixture and fried shrimp. Stir to combine, until the shrimp and walnuts are evenly coated with the mayonnaise mixture. Top with the green onions. Serve immediately.

SERVES 2

12 classic fried shrimp (page 75), warmed

2 tablespoons honey

½ cup walnut pieces

1 cup vegan mayonnaise

3 tablespoons agave nectar

¼ cup sliced green onions

MAFIA MOBSTA NOODLES

aka Garlic Noodles

Garlic noodles is real mob, so I had to put this on the menu. In the culture, you're eating good whenever you get to eat this dish. It feels real fly and player, especially with crab or seafood on top. This was one of my favorite things to eat before I was vegan, so when I went plant-based, I knew I had to make a version that was just as good but didn't have oyster sauce, butter, and all that. It was a big hit. These make a great dinner when you add vegan fried shrimp (page 98) and some of Uncle Mobby's Green Beans (page 123). Or try with Blazin' Chili-Garlic Dipping Sauce (page 142).

1 — Heat the olive oil in a large wok over medium heat for 1 minute. Add the vegan butter and let it melt.

2 — Add the garlic and stir-fry for 2 minutes so garlic is cooked and fragrant but not browned.

3 — Add the cooked noodles and toss to combine with the butter and oil. Add the soy sauce and toss to coat noodles. Let cook for 2 minutes, until warmed.

4 — Add the parsley and grated vegan parmesan and toss to combine. Serve immediately.

SERVES 4

2 tablespoons olive oil

1 tablespoon vegan butter, preferably Earth Balance

3 garlic cloves, chopped

1 (16-ounce) package pre-cooked vegan yakisoba noodles, or 3 cups other cooked vegan Asian-style noodles, such as ramen (about 6 ounces uncooked)

¼ cup chopped fresh parsley

½ cup soy sauce

½ cup grated vegan parmesan, preferably Follow Your Heart

SHRIMP FRIED RICE

Growing up I loved shrimp fried rice and would always order it when we got Chinese food. There was a restaurant called Peking Restaurant in my neighborhood and, to me, it was the best Chinese food in the world. It wasn't gourmet; it was just really good, tasty food. Eating at that spot made me fall in love with shrimp fried rice. When I think of this dish, I think of my momma feeling good and wanting to splurge on dinner for us at Peking. This is the vegan version of that dish with similar flavors. When you're picking a vegan shrimp, soy shrimp work best for a dish like this one since you're not coating and frying them. I like to use the brand Tôm Nguyên Con, which you can order online. If you can't find that, you can use BeLeaf vegan shrimp.

1 — In a large wok, melt the butter over medium heat. Add the garlic and sauté until the garlic is fragrant but not browning, about 2 minutes.

2 — Add the olive oil and mix with a rubber spatula.

3 — Add the carrots, onion, peas, vegan shrimp, green onions, and salt and sauté for 6 minutes, until the carrots are tender, being sure not to let the vegetables brown.

4 — Add the rice to the pan and mix, using a rubber spatula to break up any clumps. Mix until the vegetables are evenly combined and the grains are coated with butter and oil. Sauté for about 4 minutes, until the rice is heated through.

5 — Add the soy sauce and mix to make sure the rice is evenly coated. Taste and adjust the seasonings, adding more soy sauce if desired. Serve immediately.

MAKES 6 CUPS (SERVES 4)

4½ tablespoons vegan butter, preferably Earth Balance

3 large garlic cloves, chopped

3 tablespoons olive oil

2 medium carrots, diced

¾ cup chopped white onion

1 cup frozen peas

1 cup (about 8 ounces) chopped vegan shrimp

3 green onions, white and green parts, chopped

1 teaspoon kosher salt

4 cups cooked white rice, chilled (day-old rice works best)

3 tablespoons soy sauce, plus more as needed

GARLIC FRIED RICE

This dish was inspired by an upscale Japanese restaurant chain called Benihana's. When I first put it on the Vegan Mob menu, I introduced it as Benihana-style rice. It's something that Black culture has embraced and really loves, so I wanted to bring that to the Vegan Mob menu. This recipe works best with day-old rice that's had a chance to dry out overnight in the refrigerator, but it'll work with freshly made rice, too.

1 — In a large wok, melt the vegan butter over medium heat and add garlic. Sauté until garlic is fragrant but not browning, about 2 minutes.

2 — Add the olive oil and mix with a rubber spatula.

3 — Add the onion, carrots, green onions, and salt and sauté for 6 minutes over medium heat until the carrots are tender, being sure not to let the vegetables brown.

4 — Add the rice to the wok and mix, using a rubber spatula to break up any clumps. Mix until the vegetables are evenly combined and the grains are coated with butter and oil. Sauté for about 4 minutes to heat the rice through.

5 — Add the soy sauce, making sure to mix again until the rice is evenly colored. Taste and adjust seasonings with more soy sauce, if desired. Serve immediately.

SERVES 4

4½ tablespoons vegan butter, preferably Earth Balance

3 large garlic cloves, chopped

3 tablespoons olive oil

¾ cup chopped white onion

2 medium carrots, diced

3 green onions, white and green parts, chopped

1 teaspoon kosher salt

4 cups cooked white rice, chilled

3 tablespoons soy sauce, plus more as needed

MOBSTA-STYLE SHRIMP BARBEQUITO

This was the first dish I tested. Once I tasted this, I knew Vegan Mob would be a hit. We actually didn't bring this on to the menu until six months after we opened, but when we did, we never looked back. This recipe uses a lot of Vegan Mob basics, and if you have them ready to go this will be ready quick.

1— Lay out the two tortillas on a work surface. Add half the shrimp, sauce, slaw, Smackaroni, and baked beans to each tortilla, keeping the ingredients to the centers of the wraps so they're easier to fold.

2— Bring the left and right sides of the wraps toward the center. From the bottom of the wraps, roll upwards. Cut each wrap in half using a serrated knife. Serve.

SERVES 2

2 (12-inch) vegan flour tortillas

10 classic fried shrimp (page 75)

1 cup Mob Sauce (page 147)

½ cup Tasha's Slaw (page 57)

½ cup Smackaroni and Cheese (page 38)

½ cup Mobba'Q Baked Beans (page 53)

WHERE'S THE BEEF BARBEQUITO

This right here is a mob favorite, one of the original Vegan Mob dishes that was supposed to be a roti, an Indian flatbread that reminded me of a burrito. I added all of my favorite soul food dishes to the wrap, and it was an instant hit. My wife ate it every day for five days straight. Serve with extra Mob Sauce (page 147) on the side.

1— Lay out the wraps on a work surface. Add half the vegan brisket, half the sauce, half the slaw, half the Smackaroni, and half the beans to each one, keeping the ingredients near the centers of the wraps so they're easier to fold.

2— Bring the left and right sides of the wraps toward the centers. From the bottom of the wraps, roll upwards. Cut each in half using a serrated knife. Serve.

SERVES 2

2 (12-inch) vegan spinach or tomato wraps

1 cup Smoked Vegan Brisket (page 37)

½ cup Mob Sauce (page 147)

½ cup Tasha's Slaw (page 57)

½ cup Smackaroni and Cheese (page 38)

½ cup Mobba'Q Baked Beans (page 53)

STEAK BARBEQUITO

These right here smackin' with a side of strawberry lemonade (page 216)!

1— Heat the olive oil in a medium saucepan over medium heat until shimmering.

2— Add the vegan steak, kosher salt, and seasoning salt and sauté for 3 minutes, until heated through. Set aside.

3— Lay the tortillas on a work surface. Add half the steak, half the sauce, half the slaw, half the Smackaroni, and half the beans to each tortilla, keeping the ingredients to the centers of the tortillas so they're easier to fold.

4— Bring the left and right sides of the tortillas toward the centers. From the bottom of the tortillas, roll upwards. Cut each in half using a serrated knife and serve.

SERVES 2

2 teaspoons olive oil

2 (7-ounce) packages vegan shredded steak, preferably Better Chew

1 tablespoon kosher salt

1 tablespoon seasoned salt, preferably Lawry's

2 (12-inch) vegan flour tortillas

½ cup Mob Sauce (page 147)

½ cup Tasha's Slaw (page 57)

½ cup Smackaroni and Cheese (page 38)

½ cup Mobba'Q Baked Beans (page 53)

DEEP-FRIED BARBEQUITO

aka Mob Chimichanga

In high school I used to eat chimichangas every day. I loved them so much I bought them in bulk from the freezer at Costco. Here in the Bay, we've called them "turf burritos" ever since E-40 dropped that lingo in a song, "turf" meaning your block, your set, where you're from. The earth is my turf, so I keep it vegan. I love my version because it's crispy and has gooey cheese.

SERVES 2

2 tablespoons olive oil

2 (12-ounce) packages vegan ground meat, preferably Impossible ground beef

1 tablespoon Let Seasonin' Be the Reasonin' Taco Spice (page 184)

1 cup water

4 slices vegan cheddar cheese, preferably Daiya cheddar-style slices, chopped

1 large tomato, finely diced

2 (12-inch) vegan flour tortillas

1 cup vegetable oil for frying

TO SERVE

Guap-amole (page 183)

Vegan sour cream, preferably Tofutti

Salsa

1— In a medium skillet, heat the olive oil over medium heat until shimmering.

2— Add the vegan ground beef and cook for 5 minutes until browned, breaking up lumps with a wooden spoon. Add the taco seasoning and mix.

3— Add the water and let simmer until the meat is tender, about 10 minutes. Set aside.

4— Warm the flour tortillas in a large skillet over medium heat, until pliable.

5— Lay the tortillas on a flat surface and fill each with half the taco meat, half the diced tomato, and half the vegan cheddar cheese.

6— Roll each by gathering left and right sides of tortillas and bringing towards the centers. Grip the bottom of the tortilla and roll towards the top.

7— In a heavy pan, heat the vegetable oil to 375°F. Line a plate with paper towels.

8— Carefully lay the burritos, seam side down, in the oil and fry until golden brown, about 2 minutes. Flip using a spatula and fry on the other side, about another minute or two. Drain on the paper towel–lined plate.

9— Serve immediately with guacamole, sour cream, and salsa.

IT'S HARD OUT HERE FOR A SHRIMP MOB TACOS

These shrimp tacos are like the po' boy (page 98) in a tortilla. You can even add a little chopped-up avocado on top. These will be a hot item at any party or potluck.

1— Heat a nonstick sauté pan over medium heat and warm the tortillas. Set aside.

2— Add 1 tablespoon of slaw to each tortilla and top each with 3 fried shrimp. Sprinkle each taco with the green onions and tomatoes.

3— Drizzle 1 tablespoon of mob sauce onto each taco. Serve immediately.

SERVES 2

4 (4-inch) vegan flour tortillas

¼ cup Tasha's Slaw (page 57)

12 classic fried shrimp (page 75)

2 green onions, white and green parts, chopped

½ tomato, diced

¼ cup Creamy Cajun Mob Sauce (page 145)

MOB TACOS

These tacos are a favorite at Vegan Mob. When I was a kid my momma's ground beef tacos were one of my favorite things to have for dinner. I would eat like ten of them. These tacos are the best in the world because they remind me of those taco nights growing up. I wanted to put them on the menu because I love eating them so much, and they've become a big hit. Customers really like the crispiness of the taco shells and the flavor of the ground "beef." You'll want to make a lot of these for your family or for your own taco night.

SERVES 4

FILLING

2 tablespoons olive oil

1 (12-ounce) package vegan ground meat, preferably Impossible ground beef

2 tablespoons Let Seasonin' Be the Reasonin' Taco Spice (page 184)

½ cup water

TACO SHELLS

2 tablespoons vegetable oil

12 (4-inch) corn or vegan flour tortillas (use your favorite)

1 (7-ounce) package shredded vegan cheddar-style cheese, such as Daiya

TO SERVE

Red taco sauce, preferably La Victoria

Vegan sour cream, preferably Tofutti

1 medium red tomato, finely diced

1 cup shredded iceberg lettuce

1 bunch green onions, white and green parts, chopped

1 ripe avocado, pitted, peeled, and sliced

1— In a medium skillet, heat the olive oil over medium heat until shimmering.

2— Add the vegan ground meat to the skillet and let brown for 5 minutes, breaking up lumps with a wooden spoon. Add the taco seasoning and stir, then cook for an additional 2 minutes until the mix is fragrant and the meat is well coated. Add the water and simmer until the meat is tender, about 10 minutes. Keep warm.

3— In a separate large skillet or sauté pan, heat the vegetable oil over medium-high heat until shimmering. Add a single tortilla and fry until golden brown, about 2 minutes. Flip and fry the other side until golden brown. Remove from the oil and top with some of the grated vegan cheese and let melt. Repeat with the remaining tortillas, adding more oil if necessary.

4— Fill each taco shell with about ¼ cup of ground meat, taco sauce and sour cream to taste, ¼ cup of lettuce, and a sprinkle of tomato and green onions. Top each taco with a few slices of avocado. Serve immediately.

MOB TACO BOWL

I call this dish "easy money" because it's easy to put together, and everybody loves it. This makes a really quick and very flavorful dinner. When you want something light—but good—you can call on this recipe. If you wanna cheat and say fuck it, skip the lettuce and eat this with some store-bought tortilla chips and extra taco sauce. Not exactly a "light snack" anymore, but still just as good.

1— Preheat the oven to 350°F.

2— Lay the tortillas on a baking sheet and coat each side with a thin layer of olive oil. Bake for 10 to 15 minutes, until golden brown and crispy.

3— In a medium skillet, heat the olive oil over medium heat until shimmering. Add the vegan ground meat to the skillet and let brown for 5 minutes, breaking up lumps with a wooden spoon. Add the taco seasoning and cook for an additional 2 minutes, until the mixture is fragrant and the meat is well coated. Add the water and let simmer until meat is tender, about 10 minutes.

4— Divide the lettuce among four bowls. Add 3 tablespoons of ground meat to each bowl and top the meat with grated vegan cheddar. Drizzle each bowl with taco sauce and top with 1 tablespoon of vegan sour cream and a few slices of avocado. Sprinkle the tomatoes and green onions over each bowl.

5— Chop the crisped tortillas into quarters and add four pieces to each bowl. Serve immediately.

SERVES 4

4 (4-inch) corn tortillas

2 tablespoons olive oil

1 (12-ounce) package vegan ground meat, preferably Impossible ground beef

2 tablespoons Let Seasonin' Be the Reasonin' Taco Spice (page 184)

½ cup water

4 cups shredded iceberg lettuce

4 ounces shredded vegan cheddar-style cheese, preferably Daiya

½ cup red taco sauce, preferably La Victoria

¼ cup vegan sour cream, preferably Tofutti

1 ripe avocado, pitted, peeled, and sliced

1 medium red tomato, small dice

1 bunch green onions, white and green parts, chopped

FRIED CHICKEN TACOS

Let's enter the world of fusion. You can be creative with these tacos. They're easy to make and the options for toppings are endless. The kids (or the kid in you) will love these with a side of our Smackaroni (page 38). Add some Strawberry Lemonade (page 216) and a nice show or a sports game and you're good to go.

1— Cut the vegan fried chicken into smaller, ½-inch pieces.

2— In a medium skillet, heat the olive oil over medium heat until shimmering. Add the chicken pieces, taco seasoning, and water. Let cook for 3 minutes, or until a sauce forms. Remove from the heat and set aside.

3— Heat the flour tortillas in a medium pan over medium heat, until warmed through.

4— Lay two tortillas on each plate. Add a spoonful of chicken and sauce to each tortilla. Top with lettuce, sour cream, guacamole, and a dash of hot sauce. Finish with green onions and tomatoes. Serve immediately.

SERVES 3

8 ounces vegan fried chicken, preferably Better Chew, thawed if frozen

2 tablespoons olive oil

2 tablespoons Let Seasonin' Be the Reasonin' Taco Spice (page 184)

½ cup water

6 (6-inch) vegan flour tortillas

½ head iceberg lettuce, shredded

Vegan sour cream, preferably Tofutti

Guap-amole (page 183)

Hot sauce

½ bunch green onions, white and green parts, chopped

1 large tomato, chopped

GUAP-AMOLE

aka Guacamole

When you're getting your "guap," it means getting your money, and this guap-amole aka guacamole is money. Serve on the side of your favorite tacos, Fire Salsa and Chips (page 199), or the Classic Mobchos (page 200).

1— Cut the avocado in half and remove the pit. Use a large spoon to remove the flesh and add to a medium bowl.

2— Add the lemon juice, cilantro, red onion, garlic powder, red pepper flakes, and salt and mix well, mashing the avocado as you go. Taste and adjust the seasonings as desired.

3— For best results, cover and refrigerate for an hour before serving.

MAKES 1 CUP

1 large avocado, as ripe as possible

2 tablespoons fresh lemon juice

½ bunch cilantro, minced

½ medium red onion, finely diced

½ teaspoon garlic powder

1 pinch red pepper flakes, plus more to taste

1 teaspoon kosher salt, plus more to taste

LET SEASONIN' BE THE REASONIN' TACO SPICE

This is the mix we use to get our vegan proteins for tacos ready to go. You can buy premade packets at the grocery store or use this mix instead, which gives you the opportunity to customize it to how spicy or how salty . . . really, however you like your tacos. Double or triple the recipe to have enough to keep on hand for taco nights.

Mix together the chili powder, garlic powder, onion powder, cumin, chipotle powder, cayenne, smoked paprika, and pink Himalayan salt in a small bowl until well blended. Use right away or store in an airtight container in a cool, dry place for up to two months.

MAKES 4 OUNCES (ABOUT ½ CUP)

2 tablespoons chili powder

2 teaspoons garlic powder

2 teaspoons onion powder

2 teaspoons ground cumin

2 teaspoons ground chipotle powder

2 teaspoons cayenne pepper

2 teaspoons smoked paprika

2 teaspoons pink Himalayan salt

"BE YOURSELF AND BE AUTHENTIC.

THAT'S HOW YOU HOST THE BEST PARTY."

I always cook extra, and I'm so used to it that I always have lots of plastic containers so people can take food home. Growing up, my family mobbed deep to my grandmother's house for holidays or just to get together, and I'd watch her put up enough food to feed an army. Big portions of all types of shit. Good-ass brisket, collard greens, potato salad, pies, mixed drinks. There'd be friends, aunts, and uncles all around making plates and talking and having a good-ass time. There was always enough for all of us to eat and be full when she cooked. Because of the pandemic, we don't do the big parties that we used to, but I still cook like that because I want the people I cook for to be satisfied and not want for anything.

That's really what you should be going for when you cook for a crowd. My style of vegan food is all about sharing, and it's perfect for a party. Vegan food can be satisfying and crowd-pleasing if you bring that attitude to it. It's not a chore to provide a lot of food for people; it's a way of taking care of the people you love.

One way I've found to make planning a party easier is to make things where you can have your people help you the day before or the morning before. If you're making a bunch of lumpia or fried chicken, have your family help you with prep so you can knock out a whole bunch in a few hours. Have a friend blend up the mixed drinks right before folks get there. Bring kids into it, too, and let them help make a dish or drink for the party. That's what makes it fun. Doing it all by yourself can be draining, but bringing other people into it, you'll make memories, and they'll feel like they helped plan the party, too.

CREATE A SPREAD

The best parties have dishes that are crowd-pleasers and a little bit of something for everyone. I've been to parties where there was no vegan food, and me and my wife had to leave early because we were hungry. Don't do that to your guests; make sure they can enjoy something in the spread. I try to pick out a variety of food, maybe eight to ten dishes, and make sure that everything is a household favorite that people love. I might do a big pot of spaghetti, some fried chicken, potato salad, some lumpia, good-ass greens, and mobby green beans. A big green salad with lots of different textures and vegetables can also be nutritious, and people love them. Make sure the vegetables taste good, just as good as the proteins.

DON'T NEGLECT TEMPERATURE

When it's time to serve the food, you can't just set it out and forget about it. Make sure you have a way of keeping hot stuff hot and cold stuff cold. Just because it's vegan doesn't mean temperature isn't a big factor in something tasting good. If you're cooking that day, keep dishes warm in the oven while you work in batches until all of the food is done. During the party, check in on the temperature of dishes and reheat them if necessary. If you put out nacho cheese, for example, you may need to periodically microwave it to make sure it's hot. Cold items can be kept on ice or covered to keep the temperature down.

CREATE A VIBE

In Black culture we show out, which is a way of saying we present our best selves. If it's a party . . . we want to show out. When you're welcoming people into your home, show out by letting them know how you get down. Think about everyone who's coming and what they need to have a good time. Don't leave anybody out—you got to take care of everybody. For me, that means have some music and have some drinks—alcoholic and nonalcoholic. The mob is going to want to eat and chill. You could have games like cards or dominoes for people to play. If there's a football or basketball game on, turn that on in the other room and make it a fun house. Have your party like your menu: everything is good, every room is poppin'.

You'll have an idea if you're throwing a good party by how people are acting and the sounds. If it's quiet and people are just sitting around, bored, then maybe you need to add some music and get people on their feet. Ask yourself what you need to have a good time and go from there.

The main thing is there's no right way. Just do it the way they would do it. If you're making the Vegan Mob recipes, make sure you match what you think would go the best. Bring your own vibe, your own flavor, and have fun. Throw on some music that you love. Put out the dishes that you love. That's how you add the flavor you love and what you think is fun. Everybody is different, so every party is going to be unique. Be yourself and be authentic—that's how you make the best party.

If I had to plan a dream party, it would look something like this: outdoors for sure, in the spring because that's my favorite season in the Bay, tables of food with garlic noodles, lumpia, Smackaroni, greens, spaghetti, candied yams, smoked brisket with Mob Sauce, and cheeseburger rolls—all from Vegan Mob, of course. I'd have plenty of peach mobbler and a whole dessert bar with candies and vegan banana pudding. There would have to be a DJ going crazy all day, playing Mac Dre, some reggae, some old-school hip-hop, 80s R&B like Bobby Brown and Rick James, just mixing it up with all the music and genres that I love. There's got to be some Earl Stevens Wine made by the Bay legend himself, E-40, for those who drink. And we'd have a bowl of that good Cali tree, that Vegan Mob exotic. We would get the party poppin' at seven or eight at night, and we wouldn't stop

until two in the morning. That's a Vegan Mob party right there. That's how we mobbin' in the Bay. That might seem late to you, but we mob a little later because a Bay party definitely don't stop.

GET YOUR DESSERTS

Desserts were a big deal in my family, not only because they were hella good but because my grandma had a sweet tooth and often made a dessert out of the blue just to have around. There was always a cake in the kitchen or some pudding made with leftover rice or bread from dinner the night before. As my mom says, it was "real country cooking" because it was about making the best thing you could, using what was around. A few eggs, some sugar, some milk, and some stale bread could become a dessert. Sometimes the rice pudding had raisins, or the bread pudding had pineapple added to it; it just depended on what was in the pantry when my grandmother made it. And there was vanilla ice cream, too, to go with it. She didn't make that though; it was always store-bought.

But it's peach cobbler that brings me right back to growing up. When I smell it, it's Christmas time and I'm young again. The smell of just-baked, buttery pie crust, canned peaches mixed with a little of their syrup or fresh peaches, and spices like cinnamon and nutmeg transports me right back to my grandmother's kitchen. We would go over to her house on Christmas Day, and the whole house would smell like that, then she'd pull the cobbler out of the oven, and it'd be bubbling and golden brown and perfect.

She didn't make it all the time, and when she did, she made it really good. A lot of peach cobblers either have dense dumplings that have soaked up the pie juices or a lot of crumbly cake on top, making it heavy. My grandmother's wasn't like that at all. Hers had a lattice top like a pie that gave it a crispy texture against the soft peaches. It tasted like heaven. It was light and syrupy but not too thick. When she used canned peaches, she'd use just a touch of the syrup from the can to make the base, mixing it with sugar and boiling it to make the filling. That recipe has been passed around in our family from my grandmother to her children and grandchildren and eventually to me, where I serve it at Vegan Mob. Listening to my mom talk about those recipes, and how much she misses my grandmother and her cooking, brings tears to my eyes.

After I went vegan and I first made the peach mobbler, it didn't even feel like I was even experimenting. I'd made it so many times with my family, and I'd seen it done so many times by the women in the family that I knew exactly what I was doing, even though I was using vegan products. When I pulled it out the oven, it came out perfect and just like I remembered. My whole apartment smelled like Christmas Day. I felt so proud that I'd made it vegan and just like I remembered. It all came together.

Sweet potato pie is another dessert I tried to make vegan one time, and it came out pretty good, but I couldn't find an egg substitute, so I used a little flour. Once I found an egg substitute, it came out just like I remember making back when I wasn't vegan. It was on point. The consistency of the filling wasn't too soft; it was firm, and we could taste the sweet potatoes with a balanced background of nutmeg and cinnamon—not too much, but just enough to break up the sweetness. The crust was crunchy on the outside, providing a little bit of texture, but not burnt.

I'm more of a savory person than a dessert person, but I live with two dessert fiends: my wife and my daughter. I have a "sometimes" sweet tooth where I get cravings for candy, or I might want a slice of apple pie or peach cobbler, but they're obsessed. If we go out to eat, they'll always make sure we get a vegan dessert. They love anything with chocolate in it. I don't typically make dessert at home unless it's a special occasion, or unless my daughter asks me to make her a chocolate cake. They mostly figure that out for themselves, and I don't trip. I get some Sour Patch Kids, Skittles, vegan gummies, or fruit chews and keep it moving.

I may not have the same sweet tooth, but I do understand how dessert can provide the perfect ending to a meal. With vegan dishes it's no different. You're still looking for the same things as a nonvegan dessert: sweet, with good texture and good flavor.

Vegan desserts don't have to be boring or simple if you treat them like that. Just because you're vegan doesn't mean that you can't have dessert that leaves you in a good mood. And there's so many products available on the market to help you make vegan desserts that taste like nonvegan desserts. Just Egg brand egg substitute, coconut whipped cream, cacao powder, peanut butter, there's even soy cream cheese for cheesecakes. There's a lot of options, and you can play with them until you find a recipe that works for you. Get creative with the substitutes. The vegan world has so many options that there's endless possibilities to create that dessert you may have had when you were not vegan.

FIRE SALSA AND CHIPS

My mom used to buy chips and Casa Sanchez salsa as her snack and hide them so I wouldn't eat it all. But I'd sneak into the kitchen at night and eat some. This is my take on that familiar taste, with a spicy kick (that's a warning) and lots of garlic and some fresh chips. The chopped cilantro adds freshness that you can't substitute. It tastes just like the authentic salsa you get at Mexican restaurants.

1 — Make the salsa: Combine the tomatoes, onion, chiles, garlic, cilantro, and salt in a blender and pulse until the ingredients are broken down but still a little chunky. Taste and adjust the salt if desired. Set aside.

2 — Make the chips: In a heavy pot or Dutch oven fitted with a thermometer, heat the vegetable oil until it reaches 375°F. Line a plate with paper towels.

3 — In batches, fry the tortilla pieces in the oil until golden brown, about 3 minutes. Remove with a spider or tongs and drain on the paper towel–lined plate. While the chips are still hot, dust with salt. Repeat with the remaining tortilla pieces.

4 — Serve the warm chips with the salsa. Leftover salsa can be stored in an airtight container in the fridge for a few days.

MAKES 2 CUPS SALSA (SERVES 6)

SALSA

3 large tomatoes, quartered

1 large white onion, quartered

2 serrano chiles, halved vertically

5 garlic cloves

1 bunch cilantro, stems trimmed, roughly chopped

1 tablespoon kosher salt, plus more to taste

CHIPS

10 yellow corn tortillas, quartered into wedges

3 cups vegetable oil

Kosher salt

CLASSIC MOBCHOS

These right here are an original "Mob classic." Basically, when you eat these, it's like being right outside of Vegan Mob. These are served buffet-style, so everyone gets what they want . . . no fighting.

1— Put the chips, cheese sauce, slaw, Mob Sauce, and Guap-amole in individual bowls, making sure the cheese sauce can be kept warm or reheated in the microwave.

2— Let guests assemble their own plates of nachos.

SERVES 4

1 (17-ounce) bag tortilla chips

2 cups Nacho Cheese Sauce (page 122), warmed

2 cups Tasha's Slaw (page 57)

1 cup Mob Sauce (page 147)

1 cup Guap-amole (page 183)

SPICY TACO MOB NACHOS

aka Fully Loaded Mob Nachos

These are my favorite nachos right here. Fully Loaded Mob Nachos was one of the first items on the Vegan Mob menu, and our customers go crazy for it. If the Classic Mobchos (page 200) are the classic, then this version is the barbecue-style, soul-food-nachos version, a whole different take on classic nachos. These fasho gonna blow yo' mind . . . wash them down with Strawberry Lemonade (page 216). It's a match made in heaven!

1 — In a medium skillet, heat the olive oil over medium heat until shimmering.

2 — Add the vegan ground meat and let brown for 5 minutes, breaking up lumps with a wooden spoon. Add the taco seasoning and cook for an additional 2 minutes, until the mix is fragrant and the meat is well-coated. Add the water and let simmer until meat is tender, about 10 minutes.

3 — Arrange the tortilla chips on a large serving platter. Top with the brisket, cheese sauce, green onions, tomatoes, and jalapeños. Place vegan sour cream, guacamole, and salsa on the sides of the platter for dipping. Serve immediately.

SERVES 4

2 tablespoons olive oil

1 (12-ounce) package vegan ground meat, preferably Impossible ground beef

2 tablespoons Let Seasonin' Be the Reasonin' Taco Spice (page 184)

½ cup water

1 (17-ounce) bag tortilla chips

2 cups Smoked Vegan Brisket (page 37), warmed

2 cups Nacho Cheese Sauce (page 122), warmed

1 bunch green onions, white and green parts, chopped

1 medium red tomato, chopped

1 (6-ounce) jar pickled jalapeños, drained

1 (12-ounce) container vegan sour cream, preferably Tofutti

1 (15-ounce) container guacamole

1 (15-ounce) jar salsa, preferably Casa Sanchez

BUFFALO CHICKEN–FRIED MUSHROOMS

This dish is for people who want some vegan buffalo wings but don't want to rock with the soy products. This will satisfy that fried chicken craving, but you're eating some good-ass mushrooms that are hella flavorful. You can serve it with Creamy Cajun Mob Sauce or, my personal favorite, Mob Ranch.

1 — Combine the Buffalo sauce and mushrooms in a large bowl and let sit for 30 minutes.

2 — While the mushrooms are marinating, combine the flour and seasoning in a large bowl.

3 — Working in batches, toss a few marinated mushrooms in the seasoned flour and lay them on a plate. Continue until all the mushrooms are coated in flour.

4 — In a heavy pan or Dutch oven, heat the oil until it reaches 375°F. Line a plate with paper towels.

5 — Working in batches, add the mushrooms to the oil and fry until golden brown on all sides, about 4 minutes.

6 — Using tongs or a spider, remove the mushrooms from the oil and allow to drain on the paper towel–lined plate.

7 — Serve immediately with Mob Sauce or Mob Ranch.

SERVES 2

2 cups Mobbin'-Ass Buffalo Sauce (page 146)

1 pound fresh oyster mushrooms, washed, split, and patted dry

2 cups all-purpose flour

3 tablespoons Creole seasoning, preferably Tony Chachere's Original

2 cups grapeseed oil for frying

Creamy Cajun Mob Sauce (page 145) or Mob Ranch (page 146) for serving

CHEESEBURGER ROLLS

These were created in my kitchen when I was living in the Dimond District. It was Christmas Day, and I had to make dinner. I thought I would try out dishes I wanted to serve on my menu one day. I was originally going for a dumpling or egg roll, so I didn't use any cheese, just the seasoned meat. My sister said it reminded her of a cheeseburger, so I reworked the recipe to include cheese. Imagine pullin' up to the Oakland Vegan Mob, hungry as hell. You gonna grab an order of these with extra Mob Ranch on the side, and you know you'll be full. People drive for hours just to get these thangs.

1— In a large bowl, combine the vegan ground beef, chopped vegan cheddar, and seasoning. Mix until well mixed. Set aside.

2— In a small bowl, mix the water with the flour until smooth. Set aside.

3— Remove the spring roll wrappers from the packaging and cut in half horizontally using a large, sharp chef's knife.

4— Separate a layer of the spring roll wrappers and place on a cutting board with the shorter side facing you. Using a tablespoon measure, place a heaping spoonful of filling 1 to 2 inches above the shorter edge of the spring roll wrapper.

5— Using your fingers, hold down the filling and lift the edge of the spring roll wrapper over the mound of filling. Roll the mixture in the wrapper until you reach about 2 inches from the end.

6— Wet your fingers with the flour-water mixture and press against the top of the wrapper to create a seal. Once a roll is sealed, place it seam-side down on a plate or baking sheet and repeat the process with remaining filling and spring roll wrappers.

MAKES 50 SMALL ROLLS (SERVES 10 TO 12)

1 (12-ounce) package vegan ground meat, preferably Impossible ground beef

1 (7-ounce) package sliced vegan cheddar-style cheese, preferably Daiya, chopped

1 tablespoon Creole seasoning, preferably Tony Chachere's Original

½ cup water

1 tablespoon all-purpose flour

1 (11-ounce) package spring roll wrappers (25 sheets), thawed, (I use O'Tasty brand, but any will do)

Vegetable oil for frying

Mob Ranch (page 146) for serving

7 — When the rolls are finished, freeze until firm, at least 4 hours.

8 — When ready to cook, heat about 4 inches of oil in a heavy pan over medium-high heat to 350°F, or until the oil is hot enough for a roll to sizzle when dropped in. Line a plate with paper towels.

9 — Fry the cheeseburger rolls in batches of five, being sure to turn so they're golden brown on each side, about 3 minutes total.

10 — Drain on the plate lined with paper towels. Repeat with the remaining rolls.

11 — Serve immediately with plenty of Mob Ranch for dipping.

LA LA LUMPIA

Being from San Francisco, I grew up around a lot of Filipinos, and I loved lumpia from the first time I had them at a get-together. Lumpia are usually made with ground pork, but I make mine with my twist, using vegan ground "beef" instead and garlic chili sauce for flavor. Whenever someone says they love my lumpia, it feels like I'm paying tribute to the people who made it for me. We show love to every culture in the Bay, and this is my homage to the Filipinos I grew up with. We call these La La Lumpia in honor of my big cousin Bax a Billion, who passed away. Bax was very important to the whole family and had a daughter named La La who he talked about constantly, so I wanted to honor that. Bax was also really important to all of us in Fillmoe. Everybody had love and respect for the Billion. He is definitely looking down on me hella proud. I can hear him right now.

1— Make the filling: In a large mixing bowl, combine the vegan ground meat, chili garlic sauce, garlic, ginger, soy sauce, green cabbage, carrot, and green onions. Mix well, making sure all the ingredients are well blended.

2— Remove the spring roll wrappers from the packaging and cut them in half horizontally using a large, sharp chef's knife, so you have 50 wrappers total.

3— In a small bowl, mix the water with the flour until smooth. Set aside.

4— Separate a spring roll wrapper and place it on your work surface, with one of the shorter ends facing you. Using a tablespoon measure, place a heaping spoonful of filling 1 to 2 inches above the edge of the spring roll wrapper nearest to you.

5— Using your fingers, hold down the filling and lift the edge of the spring roll paper over the mound of filling. Roll the mixture in the wrapper until you reach about 2 inches from the end of the wrapper.

CONTINUED

MAKES 50 LUMPIA (SERVES 10 TO 12)

FILLING

1 (12-ounce) package vegan ground meat, preferably Impossible ground beef

2 tablespoons garlic chili sauce

3 tablespoons minced garlic

3 tablespoons peeled and minced fresh ginger

3 tablespoons soy sauce

3 cups thinly sliced green cabbage

½ cup grated carrot

½ cup chopped green onions, white and green parts

1 (11-ounce) package spring roll wrappers, 25 sheets, defrosted, (I like O'Tasty brand, but any will do)

½ cup water

1 tablespoon all-purpose flour

Vegetable oil for frying

Sweet chili sauce for dipping

LA LA LUMPIA,
CONTINUED

6 — Wet your fingers with the water-and-flour mixture and press against the top of the wrapper to create a seal. Once the lumpia are rolled, place seam-side down on a plate or baking sheet and repeat the process with the remaining filling and spring roll wrappers.

7 — Heat about 4 inches of oil in a heavy pan over medium-high heat to 350°F. Line a plate with paper towels. When the oil reaches 350°F or is hot enough that lumpia sizzle when dropped, fry the rolled lumpia in batches of five, being sure to turn so they're golden brown on each side, about 3 minutes. Drain on the paper towel–lined plate. Repeat with the remaining lumpia. Do not allow the oil to get so hot it smokes.

8 — Serve immediately with sweet chili sauce for dipping.

JALAPEÑO MOBSTA POPPERS

I loved eating jalapeño poppers when I was nonvegan, so I wanted to make my own version. This recipe makes creamy, spicy jalapeño poppers that are perfect appetizers. Really satisfying and hit the spot. Put these on a platter and pair with some ranch dressing or some vegan sour cream for dipping. Fire!

1— Cut the vegan cheddar into 1-inch-wide rectangular strips. Make sure you have 24 strips.

2— Use your left hand to hold a jalapeño by the stem. Using a paring knife, slice each pepper in half horizontally. Remove the seeds and inner membranes.

3— Fill each half with a strip of vegan cheddar. Set aside.

4— Make the batter: In a medium bowl, stir together the water, flour, Cajun seasoning, salt, and pepper until smooth.

5— Place the panko breadcrumbs on a plate.

6— Working in batches of four, dip each jalapeño half into the batter. Then roll the dipped jalapeños in the panko crumbs to coat all over. Set on a half sheet pan or dinner plate. Repeat until all are coated.

7— Freeze the jalapeño poppers until firm, about 1 hour.

8— Heat at least 3 inches of vegetable oil in a heavy pot or Dutch oven to 350°F. Line a plate with paper towels.

9— When the oil is hot, add the jalapeños in batches of five and fry until golden brown, about 5 minutes. Drain on the paper towel–lined plate. Repeat with the remaining jalapeños.

10— Serve immediately with Mob Ranch sauce for dipping.

MAKES 24 POPPERS (SERVES 8)

2 (7-ounce) packages vegan cheddar cheese slices, preferably Daiya cheddar-style slices

12 whole jalapeños

2 cups panko breadcrumbs

Kosher salt

Vegetable oil for frying

Mob Ranch (page 146) for serving

BATTER

2 cups water

1 cup all-purpose flour

2 tablespoons Cajun seasoning, preferably Slap Ya Mama

1 teaspoon kosher salt

1 teaspoon freshly ground black pepper

WATERMELON AND LIME PUNCH

A good-ass punch made with fruits. Hella good on a hot day!

1 — Combine the watermelon, lime juice, and sugar in a blender and pulse until smooth.

2 — Taste and adjust sweetness with additional sugar, if desired.

3 — Chill in the freezer for several hours, until ice cold but not frozen.

4 — Serve ice cold.

MAKES 4 CUPS (SERVES 4)

½ medium watermelon, rind removed, seeded, and chopped

½ cup fresh lime juice

½ cup granulated sugar, plus more to taste

PEACH AGUA FRESCA

This is some West Coast vibes, straight up. Add some ice and just chill and sip.

1 — Combine the canned peaches and their syrup, fresh peaches, lemon juice, water, and sugar in a blender and pulse until smooth.

2 — Transfer to a bowl or pitcher and chill for several hours before serving.

MAKES 4 CUPS (SERVES 4)

1 (15-ounce) can halved peaches in syrup

2 medium fresh peaches, pitted and sliced

1 cup fresh lemon juice

1 cup water

½ cup granulated sugar

STRAWBERRY LEMONADE

People can't get enough of this drink. It's so good that we bottle it at the shop. Make it yourself—I just gave you the game. Hella smackin'!

1— Combine the strawberries, lemon juice, water, and sugar in a blender. Puree until the strawberries are broken down.

2— Pour into a pitcher and chill in the fridge until cold, at least 2 hours.

3— Serve cold.

MAKES 4 CUPS (SERVES 4)

16 ounces fresh strawberries, stemmed

1 cup fresh lemon juice

1 cup water

½ cup granulated sugar

PEACH AND BLACKBERRY SLUSHEE

Drink this as is or add some E. Cuarenta tequila and make
a mob-arita!

1— Combine the peaches, blackberries, sugar, and ice in
a blender and puree until the mixture is slushy.

2— Serve immediately or keep in the freezer until you are
ready to serve.

MAKES 4 CUPS (SERVES 4)

1 (15-ounce) can peaches in juice,
drained and juice reserved

16 ounces fresh blackberries

3 tablespoons granulated sugar

2 cups crushed ice

PEACH MOBBLER

This is my grandma's recipe—okay, maybe not to a tee, but it's how I remember it. This version has an extra dose of deliciousness because of the cinnamon and sugar on top of the flaky crust. My grandmother used to serve it with vanilla ice cream so that's how I always serve it.

SERVES 6

FILLING

1 (29-ounce) can sliced peaches in heavy syrup, drained

1 cup granulated sugar

½ stick (4 tablespoons) vegan butter, preferably Earth Balance

1 teaspoon grated or ground nutmeg

CRUST

Flour, for dusting

2 (16-ounce) frozen vegan pie shells in pans, thawed

¼ cup granulated sugar

½ teaspoon ground cinnamon

½ stick (4 tablespoons) vegan butter, preferably Earth Balance, sliced into 1-inch pats

Vanilla ice cream for serving

1— Make the filling: In a large saucepan, combine the sliced peaches, sugar, vegan butter, and nutmeg over medium heat. Stir to combine. Cook for 10 minutes, or until the sugar and butter combine to create a syrup. Set aside to cool completely.

2— Make the crust: Lightly dust your work surface with flour. Remove one of the pie shells from the baking tin and lay it on the floured surface. Using a paring knife, cut the crust horizontally into 1-inch strips. Set aside.

3— Preheat the oven to 350°F.

4— Pour the cooled peach filling into remaining pie shell.

5— Using both hands, lay one pie crust strip horizontally across the pie filling about 1 inch from the top of the pie. Repeat 1 inch below the strip with another piece. Repeat until you've reached the bottom of the pie. You should only need four strips.

6— Lay the remaining pie strips across the pie filling vertically, leaving 1 inch of space between each strip. The pie top should be in a lattice pattern when finished.

7— In a small bowl, mix the sugar and cinnamon. Sprinkle the pie with the cinnamon-sugar mixture and top with the pats of butter, evenly dispersed over the pie.

8— Set the pie on a baking sheet and place in the oven. Bake for 30 minutes, or until the crust is golden brown.

9— Let cool to room temperature, about 1 hour.

10— Serve with vanilla ice cream.

COCONUT BANANA PUDDING

Banana pudding was a must on holidays, but this version is special because I incorporated my favorite cookies, Nutter Butters. My grandma would probably be upset about this because it switches up tradition, but I had to add my swag to it. I recommend you make a batch of this for the holidays or when you are having a get-together and want an easy dessert.

1— In a large bowl, whisk together the instant pudding mix, pea milk, and vegan coffee creamer until smooth. Chill in the refrigerator until set, at least a couple of hours or overnight. Transfer the set, chilled pudding into a 9 by 13 baking dish.

2— Push cookies in vertically along the sides of the serving dish, like a fence around the edge. Then, add a layer of banana slices to cover the top of the pudding. Top the banana slices with ⅓ of the whipped topping, followed by another single layer of banana slices. Add another ⅓ of the whipped topping, followed by a layer of cookies and any remaining bananas. Spread the remaining whipped topping on top of the bananas. Top the whole pudding with the shaved coconut.

3— Chill for at least 2 hours, then serve.

SERVES 10

2 (5-ounce) packages instant vegan vanilla pudding mix, such as Jell-O

2 cups unsweetened pea milk, preferably Ripple

1 cup vegan coffee creamer, preferably Mocha Mix

1 (16-ounce) package Nutter Butter cookies

1 (9 ounce) container vegan whipped topping, thawed, preferably Sprouts Oatmilk Whipped Topping or So Delicious CocoWhip

4 bananas, sliced into ¼-inch rounds

¾ cup sweetened flaked coconut

MATTIE'S SWEET POTATO PIE

My grandmother Mattie gave sweet potato pies at the holidays. She would make a dozen or so of these pies for family, friends, and neighbors. This recipe is actually just like the one she made, but it's vegan. As it bakes, your kitchen will smell like my house smelled when I was growing up. Back in the day, I used to put Cool Whip on top, but you can use oat milk whipped cream on top, and you'll be in heaven!

1— Preheat the oven to 350°F.

2— Bake the sweet potatoes until soft, about 1 hour. Leave the oven on.

3— Let the sweet potatoes cool completely. Cut in half lengthwise. Using a spoon, scoop the flesh into a medium bowl.

4— Mix the cooled sweet potato with the egg substitute, vegan creamer, cinnamon, and nutmeg, until smooth.

5— Spoon into the pie shell and smooth the top using a rubber spatula.

6— Bake until the pie crust is golden brown and the pie filling has darkened, about 35 minutes.

7— Remove from the oven and let cool completely, about 2 hours. Slice and serve.

SERVES 6

3 large sweet potatoes

½ cup vegan egg substitute, preferably Just Egg

½ cup vegan coffee creamer, preferably Mocha Mix

1 teaspoon ground cinnamon

½ teaspoon ground nutmeg

1 (9-inch) frozen vegan pie shell, thawed

OUTRO:
BRINGING VEGAN
MOB TO THE WORLD

My friend E-40, a Bay Area legend, told me something recently that blew my mind. He told me that he bought a vegan egg substitute and used it to make an omelet for himself. He's OG from Vallejo, but he has roots in the South, and he loves soul food like fried chicken and is a big meat eater, so I was surprised when he told me. I was even more surprised when he told me why: he saw me do it on Instagram and decided to try it. "You make this shit look fun," he said.

When I think about the future of Vegan Mob, I think it's in being able to inspire people to be plant-based. I want to have Vegan Mob be an internationally recognized company that is speaking to communities of color and encouraging them to try being plant-based without giving up the foods that they love.

I feel like it's clearly working, because I see the impact of me sharing my story in real time. People walk up to me and say they went vegan because they saw me do it and share my story on social media. Young cats who aren't even twenty-five yet are going vegan and telling me about how they're choosing a healthier path in life beyond their food. I'm a role model to them because I'm from the hood, too, and they can do something positive and get good feedback. That right there is a dream, a priceless feeling that nothing can touch. I want to be financially successful, of course, but to be influential is a big goal for me and was back when I was starting out.

Looking back on some of my music, I realize I had negative influences on people before and was reaching them but leading them the wrong way. It's hard to explain it, but I know I'm doing the right thing because I'm doing all of my callings at once: cooking, music, leading, and inspiring others.

That's not to say it's been all roses. I've dealt with pain in this business: it gives me stress; it keeps me up at night. But I'm learning how to deal with this stuff and have faith. I'm also learning to not take it

GARLIC RICE

FAMILY PACKS/ PARTY TRAYS

FULL SIZE

$50.00 HALF PACK

GUMBO BUCKET

support
black
owne
bus

so seriously, because mistakes will be made. But I aim to take it seriously enough to get better at it at the same time.

The future of Vegan Mob is global. I want to franchise the business so it can be everywhere. It has to be. I know other people believe it has to be, too. Vegan Mob started as my dream, but it's become the dream of other people, too. When people tell me that I've inspired them to get up and go do something like start a business of their own or start manifesting, I love that. I love seeing people win. If I can help others find their vision and be successful, that'll be an accomplishment for me, too, even though I didn't do anything. It's about so much more than food. There's so much that's a part of the mob.

And that's what I hope this book does for you, too. I hope it inspires you to get in your kitchen, get in your community, spend time with your family. This book is about looking at your own journey and finding a calling that pulls all of the influences of your life together.

Wherever you do your thing, get busy and do your best. It's da mob.

@OFFICIALVEGANMOB
IT'S

VEGAN MOB RESEARCH AND CITED SOURCES

Congress.gov. 2021. *Congressional Record Extensions of Remarks Articles*. [online] Available at www.congress.gov/congressional-record/2009/02/26/extensions-of-remarks-section/article/E463-2 [Accessed July 19, 2021].

Dundon, Rian. "Gorgeous Photos from the 'Harlem of the West' Show the Glory Days of the San Francisco Jazz Scene." *Medium*, Timeline, May 17, 2017, timeline.com/gorgeous-photos-from-the-harlem-of-the-west-show-the-glory-days-of-the-san-francisco-jazz-scene-a42fa4f1b0cd.

"The Dust Bowl, California, and the Politics of Hard Times." *State of California Capitol Museum*, 2022, www.capitolmuseum.ca.gov/exhibits/the-dust-bowl-california-and-the-politics-of-hard-times.

"Fillmore District, San Francisco." *Wikipedia*, Wikimedia Foundation, Dec. 23, 2020, en.wikipedia.org/wiki/Fillmore_District,_San_Francisco.

"Key Findings About U.S. Immigrants." *Pew Research Center*, 2022, www.pewresearch.org/fact-tank/2020/08/20/key-findings-about-u-s-immigrants.

Kopf, Dan. "The Great Migration of African Americans to the Bay Area." The Golden Stats Warrior, Feb. 26, 2020, https://goldenstatswarrior.substack.com/p/the-great-migration-of-african-americans.

"Oakland California." *Wikipedia*, Wikimedia Foundation, May 10, 2011, en.wikipedia.org/wiki/Oakland_California.

Simley, Shakirah. "The Harlem of the West: What's to Become of The Fillmore?" *Bon Appétit*, June 6, 2018, www.bonappetit.com/story/harlem-of-the-west-fillmore.

Whitney, Todd. "A Brief History of Black San Francisco." KALW. KALW- San Francisco. https://www.kalw.org/post/brief-history-black-san-francisco. [Accessed Dec. 27, 2020]

Zito, K., 2021. Mattie Jackson, community advocate, dies. [online] SFGATE. Available at www.sfgate.com/bayarea/article/Mattie-Jackson-community-advocate-dies-3250235.php.

ABOUT THE AUTHORS

Toriano Gordon is a devoted father and husband from San Francisco's Fillmore District. After dedicating a decade of his life to helping at-risk and formerly incarcerated youth in the San Francisco Bay Area, he decided to pursue his lifelong passion of cooking. Toriano experienced a huge shift in his health and well-being after adopting a plant-based diet, and he now feels compelled to share this with others. He is the owner and founder of Vegan Mob.

Korsha Wilson is a food writer and podcast host living in the New York City area. She has written for the *New York Times*, *Saveur*, *Food & Wine*, *The New Yorker*, *Eater*, and more.

ACKNOWLEDGMENTS

First and foremost, I would like to thank my lord and savior, Jesus Christ, because without God none of this would be possible. I want to thank my wife, Maya Cameron-Gordon, for being my backbone and right hand, and my daughters, Amina and Amira, for being my number one fans. I would also like to thank my mother, Gail Jackson McCray, and all of my parents who played a part in who I am, as well as my younger sisters, Angelique and Taja Boccara, and my younger brothers, Marco Boccara and Damarco Reed. I would like to give a big wooo cooo out to the whole Fillmoe mayne, we're stronger together. I would like to give a special thanks to all of my fans. Without y'all it would be a stall. I also would like to thank the Penguin Random House and Ten Speed Press teams, my agent, Michele Crim, and my co-writer, Korsha Wilson. This greatness was a team effort. This book is dedicated to my grandmother, the late great Mattie Jackson, and my great aunts and uncles. Without them there would be no Vegan Mob!!!

This is just the beginning, there's way moe to do!

INDEX

Published in the United States by Ten Speed Press, an imprint of the Crown Publishing Group, a division of Penguin Random House LLC, New York.
TenSpeed.com

Ten Speed Press and the Ten Speed Press colophon are registered trademarks of Penguin Random House LLC.

Typefaces: Pangram Pangram's Neue Machina, and Luzi Type's Messina Sans

Library of Congress Cataloging-in-Publication Data
Names: Gordon, Toriano, 1979- author.
Title: Vegan mob : vegan bbq and soul food / by Toriano Gordon with Korsha Wilson ;
   photographs by Ed Anderson ; illlustrations by Photo Doctor Graphics.
Description: Emeryville : Ten Speed Press, 2024. | Includes index. |
   Summary: "Discover more than 80 recipes for mouthwatering plant-based fast food
   from the cult favorite Oakland BBQ joint Vegan Mob"— Provided
   by publisher.
Identifiers: LCCN 2023028006 (print) | LCCN 2023028007 (ebook) | ISBN
   9781984859969 (hardcover) | ISBN 9781984859976 (ebook)
Subjects: LCSH: Vegan cooking. | Barbecuing. | LCGFT: Cookbooks.
   Classification: LCC TX837 .G656 2024 (print) | LCC TX837 (ebook) | DDC
      641.5/6362—dc23/eng/20230623
      LC record available at https://lccn.loc.gov/2023028006
      LC ebook record available at https://lccn.loc.gov/2023028007
      Hardcover ISBN: 978-1-9848-5996-9
      eBook ISBN: 978-1-9848-5997-6

      Printed in China

      Editor: Kelly Snowden | Production editors: Ashley Pierce and
      Allie Kiekhofer | Editorial assistant: Gabriela Ureña Matos
      Designer: Annie Marino | Production designer: Faith Hague
      Production manager: Serena Sigona | Prepress color manager: Jane Chinn
      Food stylist: Lillian Kang | Food stylist assistant: Page Arnett
      Copyeditor: Andrea Chesman | Proofreader: Allison Kerr Miller
      Indexer: Ken DellaPenta
      Publicist: Kristin Casemore | Marketer: Brianne Sperber

         10 9 8 7 6 5 4 3 2 1

         First Edition